Standing Firm

When You'd Rather Retreat

Based on I Thessalonians

GENE A. GETZ

Regal Books

A Division of GL Publications.
Ventura, California, U.S.A.

Rights for publishing this book in other languages are contracted by Gospel Literature International (GLINT) foundation. GLINT also provides technical help for
the adaptation, translation, and publishing of Bible study resources and books in
scores of languages worldwide. For further information, contact GLINT, Post
Office Box 6688, Ventura, California 93006, U.S.A., or the publisher.

Published by Regal Books
A Division of GL Publications
Ventura, California 93006
Printed in U.S.A.

Any omission of credits or permissions granted is unintentional. The publisher
requests documentation for future printings.

Library of Congress Cataloging in Publication Data

Getz, Gene A.
    Standing firm when you'd rather retreat.

    1. Bible. N.T. Thessalonians, 1st—Commentaries. 2. Christian life—1960-
    . I. Title.
BS2725.3.G48   1986   227'.81077   86-429
ISBN 0-8307-1093-0

TABLE OF CONTENTS

Renewal: A Biblical Perspective   4

Introduction: Standing Firm When You'd Rather
                      Retreat   6

1. A Maturing Church   7

2. A Dynamic Witness   21

3. A Dynamic Example   33

4. Paul's Subtle Defense   45

5. A Powerful Communication Model   59

6. The Word of God   71

7. Paul's Emotional Experiences   83

8. Living to Please God   101

9. Paul's Words of Encouragement   117

10. The Day of the Lord   129

11. Roles and Relationships   141

12. Paul's Final Instructions   155

Renewal:
A Biblical Perspective

Renewal is the essence of dynamic Christianity and the basis on which Christians, both in a corporate or "body" sense and as individual believers, can determine the will of God. Paul made this clear when he wrote to the Roman Christians—"be transformed by the *renewing of your mind*. Then," he continued, "you will be able to test and approve what God's will is" (Rom. 12:2). Here Paul is talking about renewal in a corporate sense. In other words, Paul is asking these Christians as a *body* of believers to develop the mind of Christ through corporate renewal.

Personal renewal will not happen as God intended it unless it happens in the context of corporate renewal. On the other hand, corporate renewal will not happen as God intended without personal renewal. Both are necessary.

The larger circle represents "church renewal." This is the most comprehensive concept in the New Testament. However,

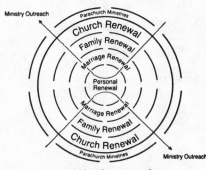

Biblical Renewal

every local church is made up of smaller self-contained, but interrelated units. The *family* in Scripture emerges as the "church in miniature." In turn, the family is made up of an even smaller social unit—*marriage*. The third inner circle represents *personal* renewal, which is inseparably linked to all of the other basic units. Marriage is made up of two separate individuals who become one. The family is made up of parents and children who are also to reflect the mind of Christ. And the church is made up of not only individual Christians, but couples and families.

Though all of these social units are interrelated, biblical renewal can begin within any specific social unit. But wherever it begins—in the church, families, marriages or individuals—the process immediately touches all the other social units. And one thing is certain! All that God says is consistent and harmonious. He does not have one set of principles for the Church and another set for the family, another for husbands and wives and another for individual Christians. For example, the principles God outlines for local church elders, fathers and husbands regarding their roles as leaders are interrelated and consistent. If they are not, we can be sure that we have not interpreted God's plan accurately.

The Biblical Renewal Series is an expanding library of books by Gene Getz designed to provide supportive help in moving toward renewal. Each of these books fits into one of the circles described above and will provoke thought, provide interaction and tangible steps toward growth. You will find a detailed listing of the Biblical Renewal Series titles at the back of this book.

STANDING FIRM WHEN YOU'D RATHER RETREAT

All of us as Christians have faced times in our lives when we'd rather turn and run away from problems and pressures. I know I have. However, to do so is not to face reality. And running from reality only makes matters worse.

The Thessalonian Christians were often confronted with incredible pressures. In fact, they were persecuted and hated, particularly by the Jewish community that resisted the gospel. Paul encouraged them to "stand firm" and not retreat. And so they did, demonstrating for Christians of all time that it is possible to be victorious in Jesus Christ.

What about you? Most of us have never faced this kind of pressure. But, we all face problems that threaten us and cause anxiety. Our natural tendency is to retreat, to go the other way.

But, in Christ, we need not retreat. We have the resources to "stand firm" in our faith and with God's help maintain both an offensive and defensive stand against Satan in whatever difficult circumstances of life we face. Thus Paul encouraged the Thessalonians to:

• Be joyful always
• Pray continually
• Give thanks in all circumstances (1 Thess. 5:16-18).

Paul's letter to the Thessalonians will help you practice these injunctions, "for," as Paul continued, "this is God's will for you in Christ Jesus" (5:18). This is *dynamic renewal* at work in our hearts and minds.

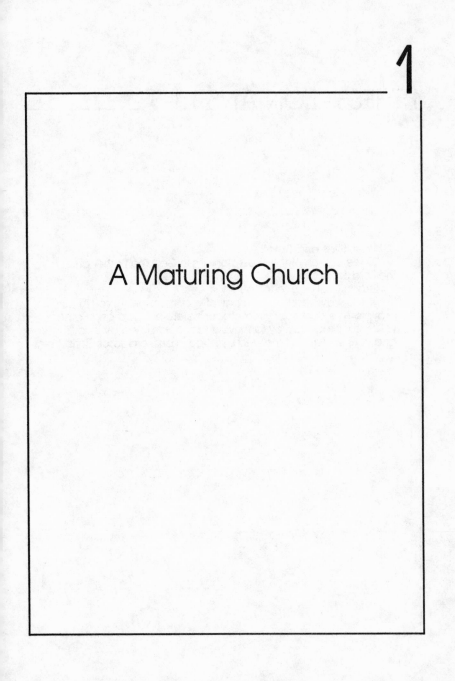

A Maturing Church

1 THESSALONIANS 1:1-3

[1]Paul, Silas and Timothy,

To the church of the Thessalonians in God the Father and the Lord Jesus Christ:

Grace and peace to you.

[2]We always thank God for all of you, mentioning you in our prayers. [3]We continually remember before our God and Father your work produced by faith, your labor prompted by love, and your endurance inspired by hope in our Lord Jesus Christ.

In the late '60s and early '70s, when I was a full-time professor at Dallas Theological Seminary, I faced some very challenging questions from my students. In general, the American society was in a state of turmoil. We were in the middle of the Vietnam War. Young people were very disenchanted with life at all levels. The "sacred cow" of science and its promised results were not working. There were no signs of the "Great Society."

Furthermore, moral and spiritual values were changing dramatically. More and more young people were becoming disillusioned with adult hypocrisy and inconsistency and were dissatisfied with what they felt was a depersonalized society that was swallowing them up, squelching their individuality and destroying their creative potential. They felt lost in a huge cultural machine that seemed out of control. They felt let down.

Their main recourse was to vent their anger on the institutions of America. They marched on Washington, staged sit-ins on university campuses and tried to burn down college buildings. They carried placards that read "Make love, not war!" Their escape was often drugs and sex.

This anti-institutional mood quickly spilled over into the religious community. The Church also became a target for severe criticism as being irrelevant, superficial and filled with hypocrisy. To many, Christian leaders were more interested in form and structure and programs than in people. Many churches were caught up in the numbers game rather than in creating an atmosphere for qualitative Christian growth.

As a professor I faced some hard questions from students who were already affected by what was happening in the society at large. And their questions forced me to ask myself some hard questions:

What does God intend the Church to be?

Why does it exist in this world?

What is its major purpose?

What is vital and dynamic Christianity?

What is the true measure of a Church?

These questions drove me to the Scriptures for a look at the New Testament churches. What were they like? What made them strong and dynamic? What made them weak and anemic?

One church impressed and encouraged me in an unusual way and helped me to discover answers to some of the tough questions—the church in Thessalonica. The city itself was a thriving commercial town located on a trade route in Macedonia. Here, Paul and his fellow missionaries, Silas and Timothy, founded the church that was destined to be one of the most talked-about churches in the New Testament world. A church born in the middle of persecution, it gloriously thrived in spite of those who tried to destroy it. Though often tempted to retreat, these Christians stood firm against the tide of worldliness and sin that constantly bombarded their lives.

THE SECOND MISSIONARY JOURNEY

Acts 15:36—16:40 provide us with the historical and geographical setting of Paul's second missionary journey (see map on following page). He and Silas had left Antioch, traveling "through Syria and Cilicia, strengthening the churches" (Acts 15:41). Eventually they "came to Derbe and then to Lystra" (16:1). There in Lystra, Paul met Timothy and invited him to join his missionary team (16:1-3).

Together, Paul, Silas and Timothy traveled from church to church, encouraging the believers. In time, they came to Troas, a seaport town on the Aegean Sea. While here Paul had a vision. He saw "a man of Macedonia standing and begging him, 'Come over to Macedonia and help us'" (16:9).

Paul knew this vision was God's call to a new mission field. He and his companions immediately boarded ship and sailed to this new area. Their first major ministry was in Philippi where they planted a dynamic church. And from there they went on to Thessalonica.

THE THESSALONIAN CHURCH

When Paul and his fellow missionaries arrived in Thessalonica, they immediately went into a Jewish synagogue (Acts 17:1-9). This practice was their normal strategy in any Roman city. Being Jews themselves, attending the synagogue gave

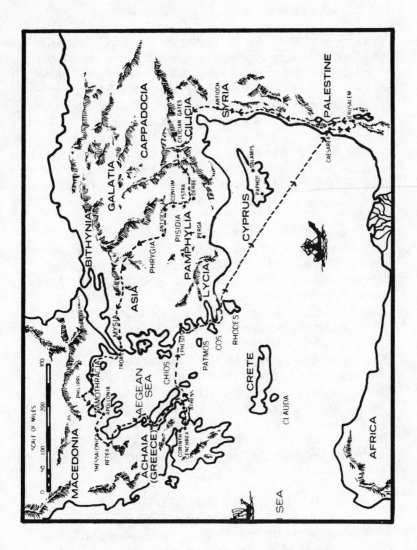

Paul's Second Missionary Journey

them a natural bridge for communicating the gospel. Using the Old Testament Scriptures, Paul explained to all who would listen that Jesus was the promised Messiah. Luke records that "some of the Jews were persuaded and joined Paul and Silas, as did a large number of God-fearing Greeks and not a few prominent women" (Acts 17:4). And so the church was born at Thessalonica.

The next events recorded by Luke involve intense persecution. As so often happened, the Jews became jealous. In fact, they were so infuriated that "they rounded up some bad characters from the marketplace, formed a mob and started a riot" (17:5).

From Luke's record it may appear that Paul and Silas left the city almost as soon as they arrived (17:10). Not so! Here is another illustration of history compressed. There is ample evidence from Paul's letter to the Thessalonians that a lot of time elapsed between verses 4 and 5 in Acts 17. These three missionaries had to have spent many days—probably months—in Thessalonica, ministering to these new believers and winning others to Christ. Their converts included not only Jews and God-fearing Greeks (Acts 17:4), but idolators as well (1 Thess. 1:9). Furthermore, Paul's reflections in the second chapter of his first letter to these Christians indicate a very in-depth teaching and discipling ministry that would have taken a lengthy period of time (1 Thess. 1:7-10). Also, the quality of these people's lives as demonstrated in this letter indicates extensive exposure to the Word of God. And this leads us to our study of the letter itself.

THE THESSALONIAN LETTER

Paul began this letter with a corporate greeting from himself and from Silas and Timothy who worked closely at his side in founding and building up this body of believers. Thus, we read, "Paul, Silas and Timothy, To the church of the Thessalonians in God the Father and the Lord Jesus Christ: Grace and peace to you" (1 Thess. 1:1).

The next paragraph in Paul's letter, following his greeting, indicates how much this group of believers had grown in their Christian lives. "We always thank God for all of you," he wrote, "mentioning you in our prayers" (1:2). He then stated *why* they were so thankful: "We continually remember before our God and Father

- your work produced by *faith,*
- your labor prompted by *love,* and
- your endurance inspired by *hope* in our Lord Jesus Christ" (1:3).[1]

We need not look far in the New Testament letters to see that *faith, hope* and *love* are the three words Paul used to describe a mature church. When Paul wrote to churches he was pleased with, he frequently began his letters by thanking God for these three qualities.

Letter to the Ephesians: "For this reason, ever since I heard about your *faith* in the Lord Jesus and your *love* for all the saints, I have not stopped giving thanks for you, remembering you in my prayers . . . . I pray also that the eyes of your heart may be enlightened in order that you may know the *hope* to which he has called you, the riches of his glorious inheritance in the saints" (Eph. 1:15-16,18).

Letter to the Colossians: "We always thank God, the Father of our Lord Jesus Christ, when we pray for you, because we have heard of your *faith* in Christ Jesus and of the *love* you have for all the saints—the *faith* and *love* that spring from the *hope* that is stored up for you in heaven and that you have already heard about in the word of truth, the gospel" (Col. 1:3-5).

Letter to the Thessalonians: "We ought always to thank God for you, brothers, and rightly so, because your *faith* is growing more and more, and the *love* every one of you has for each other is increasing" (2 Thess. 1:3).

Letter to Philemon: "I always thank my God as I remember you in my prayers, because I hear about your *faith* in the Lord Jesus and your *love* for all the saints" (Phil. 1:4-5).

When Paul mentioned these three qualities in writing to the Thessalonians he was more descriptive than usual. He actually used words demonstrating that these qualities are measurable.

Your Work Produced by Faith

Faith is a measurable quality. It produces work. It is not based on naiveté, but it does involve trusting God for what may seem an impossibility.

In America, we Christians actually know little about faith. In fact, if we removed faith from our theological vocabulary— excluding our salvation experience, would it really make much difference in the way we live? Most of us are so surrounded by opportunities that there isn't much we can't achieve on our own. Therefore, faith oftentimes becomes a concept that is difficult for us to comprehend.

This was not true among many New Testament Christians. They had no choice. They had to trust God day-by-day with their lives, for their sustenance and for the ability to help others who were just as needy as they were. And God honored their faith. The Thessalonians, we will see, were a model church in demonstrating this kind of faith.

Your Labor Prompted by Love

Love is an action word. It involves far more than feelings and compassion. It too is measurable in a church. Note the following ways in which Scripture indicates that we demonstrate love:

- Love causes us to do our part in building up the Body of Christ (Eph. 4:16).
- Love serves others (Gal. 5:13).
- Love bears with others (Eph. 4:2).
- Love helps carry another person's burden (Gal. 6:2).
- Love encourages others (1 Thess. 5:11).
- Love submits to others (Eph. 5:21).
- Love forgives (Eph. 4:32).
- Love offers hospitality (1 Pet. 4:9).

In the New Testament more is said about love than about any other quality. This is why Paul said to the Corinthians: "And now these three remain: faith, hope and *love*. But the greatest of these is *love*" (1 Cor. 13:13).

Your Endurance Inspired by Hope

Hope indicates stability. It is reflected in a body of believers who are not tossed here and there by every wind of doctrine (Eph. 4:14). It is what enabled Paul to face persecution and even death. It also enabled the Thessalonians to face persecution undaunted. And it will enable Christians everywhere to face the difficulties of life, knowing that Jesus Christ will never leave them nor forsake them. Though life may bring vicissitudes and challenges, hope perseveres and endures in the lives of mature Christians.

During a coffee break at a special conference where I was speaking, I was seated at a table listening to a very intense conversation. Several of the conferees were discussing the direction of American society—its changing moral values, its increasing crime rate, the problems in public schools, etc.

One man's response was anger. He was tempted to buy a gun and eliminate his humanistic enemies—a non-Christian reaction to say the least. One person—a woman—was demonstrating a lot of fear. She was terribly frightened about her future, her family's future and those happenings yet to occur in the future. Hers were certainly legitimate concerns.

After listening for a while, I casually inserted a comment. "If you think it's bad now, just wait," I said. "It's going to get worse."

The woman, who was scared already, looked at me—stunned! I hadn't contributed much to her sense of security with that comment! But when she regained her composure, her question was, "God wouldn't let that happen in America, would He?"

"I hope not," I responded. "But why wouldn't He?"

I went on to point out that if America did not destroy itself, it would be the first time in history that God didn't allow a nation to deteriorate and collapse when it departed from His standards of righteousness.

Don't misunderstand. I love America. And I hope the Lord will preserve our freedom for a long time—for me *and* my children to enjoy. But so often Christians living in America forget that this is really not our home. Our citizenship is in heaven. We are just strangers passing through.

Many of us have misplaced our hope. We've settled in. Our sense of security is in what we have—our freedom, our material possessions, our jobs, our families and so on.

But this was not true of the Thessalonian believers. They lived in the midst of persecution. They never knew when they might be jailed—or even killed. At any moment they could have lost everything they owned. That's why the second coming of Christ meant so much to them. Their hope was in Christ—in Christ alone. And this hope gave them a sense of security no matter what happened to them personally or to the things they had accumulated.

So it should be with us! Our hope should be in the Lord—not in our American society and all of its earthly blessings.

A CORPORATE MANIFESTATION

Note that Paul used plural pronouns in describing these qualities. He wrote: *"Your* work produced by faith, *your* labor prompted by love, and *your* endurance inspired by hope" (1 Thess. 1:3).

These qualities are marks of maturity within a group of believers—not just *personal* qualities. The facts are that personal faith and hope and love cannot be manifested effectively apart from involvement with others. This indivisibility is the uniqueness of the Body of Jesus Christ. The sum of its parts gives the Church power and dynamic visibility in the world.

Not every believer will perform at the same level. Some members of the Body may be very weak in faith, others may lack love and still others may be wavering in their hope. But together we can help each other grow and mature in our Christian lives as a corporate Body of believers.

The truth is that the fastest way for a new Christian to grow is to associate with a growing and mature church. That is why we should "not give up meeting together, as some are in the habit of doing, but let us encourage one another" (Heb. 10:25).

One afternoon I boarded an airplane in Los Angeles headed for Dallas. I thought I recognized one of the flight attendants—a young woman who had come to Christ a couple of years before. But when she saw me and recognized me I sensed some ambivalence. She was glad to see me, yet she remained reserved—a result, I later discovered, of guilt and some embarrassment.

"Where do you live now?" I asked.

She responded.

"Where do you go to church?" I asked.

She hesitated and then said, "I'm not going."

"Can we talk later?" I asked.

She was willing and later, after she had cared for the other passengers, she came and sat down beside me. After a bit of chitchat, I came right to the point.

"How's your spiritual life?" I asked.

"Not so good," she said.

And then a few moments later, she confessed she was trapped in an illicit relationship and couldn't seem to break out of it. At that moment her eyes filled with tears. Her heart was sensitive and warm.

I took her to the Galatian letter where Paul instructs those who are spiritual to help those who are caught in sin, but to do so with gentleness and humility, considering themselves lest they also be tempted (Gal. 6:1). "Carry each other's burdens," Paul wrote, "and in this way you will fulfill the law of Christ" (6:2).

I pointed out that we need each other as Christians. There are times we do get trapped in a web of sin and can't break away by ourselves. We need a loving, helping hand.

She agreed and determined to take the right step. And I'm happy to report that she did. Within a couple of weeks she was back worshiping with other Christians.

And so it is in the area of faith and hope and love. When a church is growing in these areas, we learn from each other. We are encouraged. We are motivated to step out and believe God, to trust Him and to be loving disciples of Jesus Christ.

THE TWENTIETH-CENTURY CHURCH

Ever since I faced those difficult questions back in the late '60s and '70s about the Church, I have had a new vision for God's people. I must admit that before that time I found myself measuring success more quantitatively than qualitatively. I was often more concerned with the means than with the ends. Since then I have attempted to focus on quality, and that is still my desire for the Church—the church I pastor and Churches everywhere.

Don't misunderstand! Success in God's work often involves quantitative measurement. The church in Jerusalem grew by leaps and bounds. Wherever there are people they must be reached if we are going to carry out the Great Commission of our Lord Jesus Christ. But, in doing so, we must keep the proper focus. The *true* measure of any church is the degree to which that group of believers is growing in faith, hope and love and reflecting those qualities to others.

If Paul sat down to write a letter to the average church—to your church—how would he begin that letter? What would he thank God for?

Would it be for the activities in the church?

Would he refer to the numerical growth?

To the finely-tuned organization?

Or even to the size of a huge edifice?

Obviously, every church will have activities. And if we are doing our job as God wants us to do, numerical growth usually follows. Furthermore, God wants everything to be done decently and in order. And it does take buildings to meet in and to carry on the work of God in our culture today. But sadly, a church can have all of these things and still lack faith, hope and love.

In reality, it doesn't take too much faith to build a huge church in our culture. It simply takes a lot of hard work! Resources are available as never before. But is that what God wants?

Furthermore, in our society many Christians have hope. However, their hope is often based on their possessions and in their abilities and in their sense of security on this earth. This certainly is not the kind of hope that God had in mind. True, it is a blessing to have a sense of security on earth. We should thank God for it. However, it is not the true mark of maturity in a church.

And what about love? True, many people are reaching out and helping others. But what is the motivation? Is it that others may truly see the love of Jesus Christ manifested in our lives as believers? Or are we perhaps motivated by what we might receive in return?

There lies before all of us a great opportunity

- to *develop* faith, hope and love;
- to *demonstrate* faith, hope and love; and
- to *disseminate* the results of these qualities throughout the world.

Note

1. From this reference onwards, all italicized words and phrases in Scripture quotations are added by the author for emphasis and clarification.

2

A Dynamic Witness

1 THESSALONIANS 1:4-6

⁴Brothers loved by God, we know that he has chosen you, ⁵because our gospel came to you not simply with words, but also with power, with the Holy Spirit and with deep conviction. You know how we lived among you for your sake. ⁶You became imitators of us and of the Lord; in spite of severe suffering, you welcomed the message with the joy given by the Holy Spirit.

The story is told of Gordon Maxwell, missionary to India, that when he asked a Hindu scholar to teach him the language, the Hindu replied: "No, Sahib, I will not teach you my language. You would make me a Christian."

Gordon Maxwell replied, "You misunderstand me. I'm simply asking you to teach me your language."

Again the Hindu responded, "No, Sahib, I will not teach you. No man can live with you and not become a Christian."[1]

Gordon Maxwell's reputation as a Christian preceded him. His very life-style attracted people to Jesus Christ. And so it was with the Apostle Paul and his two missionary companions, Silas and Timothy. Saint Francis of Assisi captured their philosophy of evangelism when he said, "It is no use walking anywhere to preach unless we preach as we walk!"

THE GOSPEL VERIFIED

When Paul later penned a letter to the church in Thessalonica, he was very confident about what had happened in this city. "Brothers loved by God," he wrote, "we *know* that he has chosen you" (1 Thess. 1:4). There was no question in the minds of Paul, Silas and Timothy that these people had experienced true conversion to Jesus Christ.

Unfortunately, we live in a society where many decisions for Christ are recorded and promoted. In fact, I was speaking with a well-known evangelist recently who said, "Gene, we've had a great series of meetings. Hundreds came to Christ."

I rejoiced in that report and I certainly don't want to be a skeptic. But, knowing what I do about this man's approach to evangelism and his preoccupation with numbers, I couldn't help but ask myself the question, "I wonder how many of these people really and truly were converted to Jesus Christ?" You see, under certain circumstances it is easy to get people to respond intellectually or emotionally to an invitation to receive Christ. As Americans we are masters at the art of manipulation. How many times do mass advertisers design promotional gimmicks to get us to buy something that we really don't need—or worse yet— something we really don't want?

The Apostle Paul was a master at communicating the gospel. He was very persuasive and he knew it was possible to gain followers whose hearts were not sincere. This even happened in Christ's ministry. There were many people who followed Him primarily because of what He did for them. This is very clear after Jesus multiplied the loaves and fishes and fed thousands of people. They continued to follow Jesus because of the food. Jesus had to admonish them, "Do not work for food that spoils, but for food that endures to eternal life, which the Son of Man will give you" (John 6:27).

A little later Jesus explained to the people what it really meant to follow Him. "Many of his disciples said, 'This is a hard teaching. Who can accept it?'" And then John recorded that "from this time many of his disciples turned back and no longer followed him" (John 6:60,66).

When it came to the Thessalonian Christians, Paul knew beyond a shadow of a doubt that their conversion to Christ was authentic. He then stated why. "Our gospel came to you not simply with words," he wrote, "but also with power, with the Holy Spirit and with deep conviction" (1 Thess. 1:5).

Here Paul was giving testimony to what we might term an "apostolic advantage." It is difficult to start a new movement—particularly one that is in almost every respect counterculture. How true that was in the New Testament world!

In the Jewish community, though the value system was similar to Christianity, there were many variances, particularly since Judaism had become intensely legalistic, works-oriented and very exclusive. But, it was also true in the Gentile community—and much more so! Christianity introduced the world to a value system that was diametrically opposed to paganism.

New Testament missionaries preached:

- Monotheism (belief in one God) rather than polytheism (worship of more than one god)
- Monogamy (a one man-one woman relationship) rather than polygamy
- A personal, living God rather than idols
- Honesty rather than dishonesty
- Nonviolence rather than violence

- Spiritual values rather than material values
- Love rather than hate
- Unselfishness rather than greed.

Consequently, when God introduced the world to a whole new value system, He designed a unique plan to verify the gospel message in its initial years. He did not expect the apostles, who were especially called and charged to lay the foundations of Christianity (Eph. 2:20), to have to rely on words alone.

Thus we read in Hebrews 2:3, "This salvation, which was first announced by the Lord, was *confirmed* to us by those [the apostles primarily] who heard him." But we also read that "God also testified to it [that is, the gospel message announced by Jesus Christ and the apostles] by *signs, wonders* and *various miracles,* and *gifts* of the Holy Spirit distributed according to his will" (2:4).

This dynamic process is illustrated again and again throughout the book of Acts. Peter testified to the reality of this statement about Jesus Christ when he said, "Men of Israel, listen to this: Jesus of Nazareth was a man accredited by God to you by *miracles, wonders* and *signs,* which God did among you through him, as you yourselves know" (Acts 2:22).

As the church grew by leaps and bounds in Jerusalem, Luke verified in his own historical account the manifestations cited in Hebrews 2:4. "Everyone was filled with awe, and many *wonders* and *miraculous signs* were done by the *apostles*" (Acts 2:43). Later, when Peter and John were miraculously delivered from prison, the Christians prayed, "Now, Lord . . . enable your servants to speak your word with great boldness. Stretch out your hand to heal and perform *miraculous signs* and *wonders* through the name of your holy servant Jesus" (4:29-30). God answered that prayer, for the place where they were staying "was shaken." Once again, "they were all filled with the Holy Spirit and spoke the word of God boldly." Luke records that "with *great power* the apostles continued to testify to the resurrection of the Lord Jesus" (4:31,33).

Paul too was an apostle. And everywhere he went among the Gentiles, God verified the message of the gospel with "miraculous signs and wonders" (Acts 15:12; 19:6). Writing to the Corinthians he reminded them that "the things that mark an apostle—*signs, wonders* and *miracles*—were done among" them (2 Cor. 12:12).

And so it was at Thessalonica. As Paul, Silas and Timothy ministered to these people, it was "not simply with words, but also with *power,* with the Holy Spirit, and with deep conviction" (1 Thess. 1:5). God bore witness to their message with "signs, wonders and various miracles, and gifts of the Holy Spirit" (Heb. 2:4).

THE GOSPEL EXEMPLIFIED

Another important factor was at work in Thessalonica in verifying the gospel. It involved the life-style of these three men. They demonstrated what the gospel had done in their own lives (1 Thess. 1:5). Paul developed this factor at length in the second chapter of this Epistle which we'll look at in future lessons.

This was a powerful combination. What these men shared was verified by God by means of "signs, wonders and various miracles, and gifts of the Holy Spirit" (Heb. 2:4). Furthermore, it was verified by a life-style that was diametrically in opposition to the pagan community and, in many respects, the religious community. In fact, without this second verification, people might respond to the gospel but not know how to live. This leads us naturally to a third observation regarding the Thessalonians' conversion to Christ.

THE GOSPEL PERSONIFIED

When the Thessalonian Christians responded to the gospel message, they "became imitators" of Paul, Silas and Timothy "and of the Lord" (1 Thess. 1:6). They personalized in their own experience what they observed. This is true conversion!

Imitation That's Real

Paul's statement in this verse introduces us to a very important sequence. These people had no idea what God was like.

Jesus Christ, who had revealed His Father (John 1:14), had already returned to heaven. But, here were men who were Christ's representatives not only in communicating the message of *how to be saved,* but in demonstrating with their lives *how to live!* They first imitated Paul, Silas and Timothy, and in doing so they imitated the Lord.

Someone has testified, "I first came to love my teacher; then I learned to love my teacher's Bible; and then I learned to love my teacher's Lord."

Henry M. Stanley, a former atheist, has given witness to the power of a life lived with Jesus Christ. He went to Africa and lived with David Livingstone for some time. He classified himself "as prejudiced as the biggest atheist in London." But, as he observed Livingstone's life day after day and month after month, he began to change.

At first he thought Livingstone was crazy. What would motivate this man to give himself so unselfishly to these forgotten people? But later he testified, "For months after we met I found myself wondering at the old man carrying out all that was said in the Bible . . . . But little by little his sympathy for others became contagious; my sympathy was aroused; seeing his piety, his gentleness, his zeal, his earnestness, and how he went about his business, I was converted by him, although he had not tried to do it."[2]

The poet, Annie Johnson Flint, has written that we are the only Bible some people ever read. And that is definitely true. If people who know you personally—people who associate with you every day—knew *nothing* about God's character, His attributes and particularly His holiness, what would they think? That is a sobering question, isn't it?

Example is a powerful means of communication for good or bad. A rather humorous story is told about a large chimpanzee in the Bronx Zoo in New York. As people stood and watched him he would suddenly take a deep breath with a marked slurping sound, then pucker his lips and let go with a spitball that would drown an unsuspecting onlooker. He came to be known in the zoo as The Spitter. In fact, people who were in the know enjoyed standing off to the side and laughing at the chimp's innocent victims. He never missed. His aim was deadly.

Where do you suppose this chimp learned the art of spitting? It certainly is not innate to chimps! But the ability to imitate is!

And so it is with human beings—and more so! We imitate attitudes and actions! In Paul, Silas and Timothy, the Thessalonians saw the image of the Lord Jesus Christ! What a responsibility—and privilege! When Paul wrote his second letter to the Corinthians, he said, "Follow my example, as I follow the example of Christ" (1 Cor. 11:1). What a challenge for every Christian today!

Acceptance with a Price

There was additional evidence that these Thessalonians' decisions for Christ were real. They not only "welcomed the message" these missionaries were teaching—they welcomed it "in spite of severe suffering" (1 Thess. 1:6). They knew they would have to pay a price for their decision. It meant persecution—perhaps imprisonment or even death! People who decide to follow Christ, knowing full well that they will be harassed and perhaps hurt, do so out of deep conviction. This is not the "easy believism" that is so prevalent in our society today.

What price does the average person pay, particularly in the Western world, for believing in Jesus Christ? Often very little. In fact, "being a Christian" may be an advantage. This is particularly true if you own your own business. As more and more people in business adopt an ethic that involves lying and cheating and deceit, people enjoy doing business with those they trust. That advantage exists because we operate in a society that permits us the freedom to practice our Christianity.

Unfortunately, there are people in our society who join a church to enhance their reputation in the community and for personal and selfish reasons. By contrast, there were often few advantages business-wise, socially and politically for becoming a Christian in the New Testament world. In fact, it was often a disadvantage in these areas. But there *was* one advantage—one that overshadowed the disadvantages. Christians experienced the "joy given by the Holy Spirit"—knowing they had eternal life *and* a new and divine purpose for living their lives in this world.

A DYNAMIC WITNESS TODAY

God has always had a plan for verifying the validity of His message to those who do not know Him in their hearts. When He spoke from Mount Sinai and revealed the Ten Commandments, He did so with a great manifestation of His power—smoke, lightning, thunder and earthquakes. He even spoke so His voice could be heard (Exod. 19:9-25).

When God sent His Son, He confirmed Christ's deity, not just with words, but with "signs, wonders and various miracles, and gifts of the Holy Spirit" (Heb. 2:4). And when He launched the Christian movement through the apostles He verified their message with the signs of a true apostle.

Today, and ever since the first century, God has had another unique plan. Jesus first unveiled it in the Upper Room when He told His disciples to love one another as He had loved them so that all men would know that they were His true followers (John 13:34-35). He unveiled it very specifically when He prayed for those same men, asking that they—and all who believed on Him through them—would be one with each other as Jesus was one with the Father.

The purpose for His prayer was so that the world might believe that Jesus is truly the Son of God (John 17:20-23). And as we read through the letters written to the churches we see this plan confirmed and verified again and again as being the primary means God wants us to use today to affirm the reality and validity of the gospel. It is the basis for being a dynamic witness in the world. It provides the backdrop against which the words we use to share the gospel take on meaning and power.

Let's summarize this concept with a series of questions and answers:

Q. Why did Christ come into this world?
A. *To be our Saviour from sin.*
Q. Why was He able to be our Saviour from sin?
A. *He was God in the flesh; the Son of God.*

Q. How did Christ verify that He was indeed one with His Father?

A. *He worked miracles.*

Q. What is Christ's plan today?

A. *Christ's plan today is that we demonstrate His deity and oneness with the Father through the love and unity in the visible Body of Christ.*

Q. Where has Satan attacked the Church the hardest all the way through church history?

A. *He has tried to destroy unity in the true Church and to simulate unity in the false church.*

I remember talking with a missionary to the Mormons in Salt Lake City. He told me an incredible story of a young man who graduated from a well-known evangelical Bible institute. His plan was to go to South America as a missionary. However, before going to the mission field, he decided to spend some time in Salt Lake City observing how the Mormons carried out their work. After observing both their personal and church lives, he decided to become a Mormon. When shocked parents and friends asked why, he responded, "I experienced more love and unity in the Mormon church than in any evangelical, Bible-believing church I've ever attended."

How tragic! It is common knowledge that the Mormons deny that Jesus Christ is God or that He is one with the Father. Yet this truth is the essence of the true gospel. Without this truth—that Jesus Christ is God—and without putting our faith in Christ, we cannot be saved. Consequently, Satan has worked hard to destroy love and unity in churches that believe and teach this truth, thus driving people away from true Christianity. Conversely, he works overtime simulating love and unity in a church that denies the deity of Jesus Christ, attracting millions of people to a false religion that offers false hope.

But this need not happen! Satan can be defeated. There can be love and unity in churches that believe in the deity of Jesus Christ and teach this glorious truth. Thus Paul wrote to the Ephesians, "Make every effort to keep the unity of the Spirit through the bond of peace" (Eph. 4:3). And in the last chapter of Ephesians, Paul carefully outlines the strategy for defeating

Satan (6:10-18). We are, as individuals and as a church, to put on the full armor of God.

We too can be a dynamic witness in our communities. We can present the gospel, not with words only, but against the backdrop of a loving, unified Body of Christians who demonstrate every day the miraculous power of God. Furthermore, we can exemplify the gospel in our personal lives, verifying that Jesus Christ is really who He said He is and that He can still change lives today. We too can attract people to Jesus Christ through the miraculous work of God's Holy Spirit who is transforming our lives both as individuals and as a local Body of believers.

Notes

1. Paul Lee Tan, *Signs of the Time* (Rockville, Md.: Assurance Publications, 1979).
2. Ibid.

3

A Dynamic Example

7And so you became a model to all the believers in Macedonia and Achaia. 8The Lord's message rang out from you not only in Macedonia and Achaia—your faith in God has become known everywhere. Therefore we do not need to say anything about it, 9for they themselves report what kind of reception you gave us. They tell how you turned to God from idols to serve the living and true God, 10and to wait for his Son from heaven, whom he raised from the dead—Jesus, who rescues us from the coming wrath.

As I was reflecting on Paul's encouraging words and positive feedback to the Thessalonian Christians regarding their dynamic example in the New Testament world (1 Thess. 1:7-10), my mind drifted back many years to the time I became a Christian. I was 16 years old and lived with my family on a small farm in Indiana. A short time after I accepted Jesus Christ as my personal Saviour, my dad approached me one day and asked me to help a neighbor shell corn. That may mean very little to anyone who has not grown up on a farm or who lives on a modern farm. Today they pick and shell corn in one operation, dry it in huge jet dryers and sell it immediately.

In those days we picked the corn in the fields and stored the ears in cribs, allowing the grain to dry out during the long winter months. Certain families operated "corn shelling" businesses. In the spring they mounted a huge machine on the back of a truck and went around to various farms. They would back their shellers up to the crib and shell the corn, charging a certain amount per bushel. That was their livelihood. Then the farmer would haul the corn off to the local grain elevators to be sold and shipped to various parts of the country. When the time came to shell corn farmers helped each other. Now it was our turn to help our neighbor, and Dad asked me to be the helper.

The young man who owned and operated the corn sheller was my senior by several years. I knew he wasn't a Christian since we grew up in the same community together and attended the same church. Though he was not openly rebellious against God, it was common knowledge he wasn't a Christian.

As a brand-new Christian I tried that day to share my faith with him. He listened for a few minutes—and then stopped me cold with a remark I've never forgotten. He reminded me that he attended the same Bible class I did, meaning that we had the same Bible teacher. He also proceeded to tell me about some business dealings he had had with that teacher—also a farmer—which, he said, were highly unethical.

His final words to me that day were penetrating and startling: "Look, Gene, I don't even claim to be a Christian, and I would never do business the way that man does business. He's dishonest. You mean to tell me he's going to heaven and I'm going to hell?" He stared at me long and hard, waiting for my answer.

My mouth was stopped. Words meant nothing. To this day, of course, I don't know for sure all that happened in their relationship—except that if that man did what this young man said he did, he *was* unethical.

That experience has come to my mind many times over the years. The lesson I learned that day is how important our Christian example is in communicating God's truth. The way I live affects not only how I communicate that truth but also how others receive it. Unfortunately, I know far more about that concept in principle than in practice. But my goal is to be consistent in my Christian life.

The power of example in modeling Christ flows through the first few verses of Paul's first letter to the Thessalonians. We've already noted that these people were initially impressed with the Christlike examples of Paul, Silas and Timothy. Consequently, Paul wrote, "You know how we lived among you for your sake." Furthermore, he continued, "You became *imitators* of us and of the Lord" (1 Thess. 1:5-6).

That sequence is important. These Christians first imitated the faith and life-style of these three missionaries, a pattern which then became the basis for imitating the Lord Jesus Christ.

THE THESSALONIAN MODEL

The modeling process did not stop with these three leaders. It continued through the Thessalonian Christians. What they saw in these men's lives was absorbed into their own lives and then exemplified to others.

Paul paid these Christians the ultimate compliment. "And so," he wrote, "you became a model to all the believers in Macedonia and Achaia" (1 Thess. 1:7).

Leon Morris calls this tribute "high praise."[1] Why? Because Paul gave this distinction to no other church. In fact, in his second letter to these believers, he again commended them because their faith was "growing more and more" and their love for each other was increasing. "Therefore," he said, "among

God's churches we boast about your perseverance and faith" (2 Thess. 1:3-4).

THE LORD'S MESSAGE

After commending these believers for being a model church, Paul became specific about their corporate witness (1 Thess. 1:8-10). Thus he wrote: "The Lord's message rang out from you not only in Macedonia and Achaia—your faith in God has become known everywhere. Therefore," Paul wrote, "we do not need to say anything about it" (1 Thess. 1:8).

A General Definition

The "Lord's message" rang out so clearly from pagan Thessalonica that Paul didn't even have to tell the story to others. Rather, as he traveled to other parts of the world, he heard the story repeated by others—probably by both Christians and non-Christians.

And what was this ringing message? Paul answers this question with a general definition: "Your *faith in God* has become known everywhere" (1:8).

A Specific Description

How was this faith in God revealed and reported? How all this came about is succinctly outlined by Paul in his answer to another question: What happened after they—the Thessalonians—were converted to Christ? He also details a specific example, but we'll look at that later. For now, we'll consider the three statements Paul makes in describing their faith.

First, they turned their back on idolatry (1 Thess. 1:9). Everywhere we go, Paul reported, people are telling us "how you turned to God from idols" (1:9). Though many of the initial converts in Thessalonica were Jews and God-fearing Greeks (Acts 17:4), the Church soon included large numbers of Gentiles who had been idol worshipers and had bowed down to false gods.

But these new Christians turned their backs on these idols as they became believers in Jesus Christ. People who purposely turned from idols in these Roman cities stood out dramatically against the backdrop of paganism. Consequently, they became a topic of conversation everywhere.

Have you ever seen people bow down to idols? I've had the privilege of conducting Church Renewal Conferences in Hong Kong. While walking along a beach area one day during such a conference I saw people bow down to a huge sea god that stood at least 50 feet tall. They were burning incense in front of this idol and saying prayers to this grotesque stone relic.

Though I am a Westerner used to a culture affected by the Hebrew-Christian tradition, I was reminded that not all people in this world are aware of the God we talk about so freely. For example, there are nearly 6 million people living on Hong Kong Island and in Kowloon—a space about the same size as the Dallas/Fort Worth Airport—and only about 4 percent worship the same God we do. Over 5½ million Chinese people in that small area of the world still bow down to stone idols. So when a person becomes a Christian in that setting, the new believer stands out in stark contrast to the surrounding idol-worshiping culture—just as did those in Thessalonica.

Second, they began to worship God (1 Thess. 1:9). Worshiping God was not a new idea in the Roman world. Anywhere a Jewish synagogue existed, some Gentiles knew at least a little bit about the God of Abraham, Isaac and Jacob. But when Gentiles began to turn to this God in large numbers their worship of Him became a talking point and, in many instances, a basis of persecution.

Several years later, turning "to God from idols to serve the living and true God" became the basis of a riot in Ephesus, where people worshiped a fertility goddess named Artemis (Diana). A silversmith named Demetrius made little statues of this goddess and developed a thriving business selling these figurines both to the Ephesians and to people who came to Ephesus from all over Asia. Because of Paul's ministry in Ephesus, so many people turned to Christ and turned their backs on this form of idolatry that Demetrius's business began to suffer. Consequently, he started a riot and it got so out of hand that Paul nearly lost his life (Acts 18:23—20:1).

When people become Christians in our culture it often involves coming to an understanding that all of us need a personal relationship with Jesus Christ. We may have believed in God for years, even worshiping Him regularly in our churches. But then one day we realized that *believing in God* and *knowing Him personally* by receiving Jesus Christ to be our Saviour are entirely different matters.

When we accept Jesus Christ in this way it may not even become obvious to those around us—unless we tell someone about it. However, in the New Testament world, when people turned to God and His Son Jesus Christ and forsook their pagan background, it was a dramatic contrast!

When I was ministering in Brazil with my good friend Jim Petersen who serves with the Navigators, I met Mario Nitzche and his wonderful family. I sat at his table and listened as he shared the story of his conversion to Jesus Christ.

When Jim first met him, Mario was a Marxist; he did not believe in God. But through a series of unusual circumstances, he agreed to study the Bible with Jim. They began in the Gospel of John. As they read together and came to the words "God" and "Christ," Mario refused even to say these words. Consequently, they substituted the letter X but kept right on reading and studying. Four years after this process started, Mario became a Christian and turned his back on atheism to follow the true and living God. What a contrast! Today Mario is in charge of the Navigator ministry in all the major cities of southern Brazil.

What Mario shared that day that impacted me the most was why he kept studying the Bible with Jim. "It was this man's relationship with his wife, Marge," Mario stated. "And with his family," he added. "I saw something in their lives I was seeking. There was reality in their relationships. I wanted what they had."

That reality in relationships led Mario to discover the reason behind it—the Lord Jesus Christ in their lives. The Thessalonians saw that same reality in the relationship among Paul, Silas and Timothy! Against that background they responded to the gospel. And they in turn became a dynamic model to others who needed Jesus Christ—just as Mario Nitzche has multiplied Jim's and Marge's ministry many, many times in his own ministry.

Third, they looked for Jesus Christ's return (1 Thess. 1:10). Not only did these pagans turn from idolatry to worship the true God, but they developed a sense of expectancy regarding the second coming of Jesus Christ. This is a vital Christian doctrine. Not only did Jesus Christ come into this world as the Son of God and die on the cross, but He was buried and arose from the dead. He then ascended to heaven, promising that He would come again.

Even before His death Jesus Christ consoled His disciples with this message of hope: "Do not let your hearts be troubled. Trust in God; trust also in me. In my Father's house are many rooms; if it were not so, I would have told you. I am going there to prepare a place for you. And if I go and prepare a place for you, *I will come back* and take you to be with me that you also may be where I am" (John 14:1-3).

This promise was particularly meaningful to New Testament Christians who were undergoing intense persecution. They looked forward to deliverance. And this is why the doctrine of Christ's second coming was so encouraging to the Thessalonian believers.

THE STRONG FAMILY

In applying this message to my own life and the life of every twentieth-century Christian, I'd like to focus on an important area—the family. True, the Church is a family—an extended family. But for the Church to be strong, it must be made up of strong family units—husbands and wives who love God and each other, fathers and mothers who model this love before their children, and children who love and respect their parents.

Strong families build strong churches. And in no place is modeling more powerful—for good or bad—than in the home. It is there we are known for what we really are. We can fool most people outside the home—sometimes for a lengthy period of time. But we cannot fool one another very long at the family level.

Let me focus a question that grows naturally out of the

Thessalonian passage we've just studied. To what extent have we as parents, particularly, "turned to God from idols to serve the living and true God, and to wait for his Son from heaven"?

"What do you mean?" you may ask. "We don't worship idols." In a sense that's true, for we don't worship idols in the same way the people did in Thessalonica. But remember, idolatry involves anything that comes before God.

With that in mind, let's ask ourselves some questions:

Do We Worship Humanistic Gods?

Paul reminded us in his Roman letter that when man departs from God's will in worship, his first step is to exchange "the glory of the immortal God for images made to look like mortal man" (Rom. 1:23). And whenever and wherever this happens, Paul continued, mankind has "exchanged the truth of God for a lie, and worshiped and served created things rather than the Creator" (1:25).

In our culture today, rather than worshiping images of people, we are more likely to worship people themselves. In recent years it seems the more sordid their life-style, the more attention they get in the press, on radio and on TV. If you talk to the media people, they'll tell you they're giving Americans what they want!

The Bible teaches that no human being must come ahead of God in terms of allegiance. This is a fine line—even in the passage we've studied. As we've seen, the Thessalonian Christians first imitated Paul, Silas and Timothy and then, through the example of these men's lives, came to know the Lord and worshiped Him. The love our children have for us as their parents must always point to the One who is greater than we—the God and Father of our Lord Jesus Christ.

Do We Serve Materialistic Gods?

Jesus said, "No one can serve two masters. Either he will hate the one and love the other, or he will be devoted to the one and despise the other. You cannot serve both God and Money" (Matt. 6:24).

Jesus is not teaching that it is wrong to have money and material things. However, He is teaching that it is easy to be more committed to what we have than to be committed to Him. All of us are aware of the fact that America is a prime environment for people from all walks of life to serve materialistic gods. The Bible calls this idolatry. If we as parents get caught up in this kind of idolatry, we are modeling a life-style before our children that will lead them into the same patterns of behavior.

One of the most encouraging things I have observed in our own children as they have grown to adulthood is their pattern of giving. We never taught any formal lessons on giving to God's work. However, over the years they were aware of our giving habits. They knew, even when they were very small and we were just beginning our family life, that we always set aside at least 10 percent for the Lord's work, and they also knew that we've increased that percentage over the years.

But the most thrilling thing to my wife and me has been to see them automatically do the same thing once they began to earn money. We have never knowingly reminded them as adults that they should give *at least* 10 percent. They have simply done so consistently. I cannot tell you how rewarding that is to a parent, especially to see them give beyond that percentage. I simply find myself saying, "Thank you, Lord."

Do We Serve Sensual Gods?

Throughout history, idolatry and immorality have always been closely aligned. To elaborate on what is happening in the American culture is not necessary. More and more we are worshiping at the shrine of sex. We bow down to male and female sex symbols while enjoying their flagrant immorality. We are a nation preoccupied with our sexuality. This too is idolatry.

To what extent as parents are we modeling the worship of sensual gods in our homes? Television, particularly with the presence of cable and satellite possibilities, is now bringing into the home flagrant sexual behavior that presents adultery, fornication and homosexuality in an approving way. And even general family programs are filled with innuendos that our small children can now begin to identify. Again, we must ask ourselves, "What are we modeling to our children?"

I am increasingly aware that Satan works his hardest in the breakdown and the breakup of Christian homes. The enemy of our soul is wise enough to know that if he can break up the home, he can weaken the Church. In fact, history records that the breakdown of the family has also been a primary factor in the deterioration of whole nations. The Roman Empire is a constant reminder of that fact.

I was startled to hear a story told by a friend of mine. A Christian was seated in an airplane beside another individual. Food was being served, but the other person wasn't eating. The Christian turned to him and in conversation discovered that this individual was fasting.

"You must be a Christian!" the Christian stated.

"Oh, no," his seatmate answered. "In fact, it's quite the opposite. I'm a Satan worshiper."

"Why then are you fasting?" asked the Christian.

The Satan worshiper replied with a shocking statement. "I and other satanists are fasting and praying for the breakup of the homes of a number of Christian leaders this year!"

Hearing that story shocked and sobered me deeply. Seeing Christian leaders whom I know end up in divorce courts has made me acutely aware that those of us in the ministry are not exempt from satanic attack. True, families are being destroyed because of what is happening in the world system. But this destruction is also happening because Satan and his cohorts are making a concerted effort to destroy us. And, because Christians are not on guard, our families are being destroyed.

Can We Resist the Enemy?

We can effectively turn back Satan's attacks in two ways:

First, be on guard! Put on the whole armor of God, not just as individuals, but as a couple and as a family. That armor is described for us in Ephesians 6:10-18.

We *are* in a spiritual battle. We must take it seriously. And, if we do, we will not be defeated by Satan and his hosts.

Second, pray—especially for Christian leaders, especially for those in the limelight. Chuck Swindoll—who had heard it from one of his radio listeners—told me this story of the Satan worshiper. As I talked with Chuck by phone, both of us were powerfully moved by the vulnerability that accompanies prominence, particularly that of a Christian leader.

Satan loves to see a Christian leader's family destroyed. Such a breakup disillusions the children. But, more than that, it also disillusions—and stumbles—a multitude of people who look to that leader for spiritual guidance.

Remain on your guard. And remember to uphold one another in prayer. The result will be strong Christians, strong families and a strong Church that—like the church of Thessalonica—will be a dynamic example.

Note
1. Leon Morris, *The Epistle of Paul to the Thessalonians* (Grand Rapids: Wm. B. Eerdman's Publishing Company, 1957), p. 38.

4

Paul's Subtle Defense

¹You know, brothers, that our visit to you was not a failure. ²We had previously suffered and been insulted in Philippi, as you know, but with the help of our God we dared to tell you his gospel in spite of strong opposition. ³For the appeal we make does not spring from error or impure motives, nor are we trying to trick you. ⁴On the contrary, we speak as men approved by God to be entrusted with the gospel. We are not trying to please men but God, who tests our hearts. ⁵You know we never used flattery, nor did we put on a mask to cover up greed—God is our witness. ⁶We were not looking for praise from men, not from you or anyone else.

I'm sure that most adults have faced, at some point in life, unjust criticism. It may be from a marital partner—which is very painful. It may be a parent facing accusation from a child. This is equally painful. It may be criticism from fellow employees where you work or from your boss. You may be a pastor or spiritual leader facing criticism from those you are trying to minister to.

In such situations it is difficult to defend yourself against unjust criticism without being defensive. What should you, a Christian, do when you find yourself in this kind of situation?

The Apostle Paul probably was accused falsely more frequently than any leader in the history of the Church. At times his apostleship was questioned. Some falsely accused him of taking advantage of people financially. At times he was even accused of sexual immorality. In fact, he was charged with all of these things because of his ministry in Thessalonica. His response in the Thessalonian letter illustrates how he handled this criticism. And his approach is so subtle that, until I began to study this letter in depth, I didn't even recognize it as a defense of both himself and his fellow missionaries, Silas and Timothy.

A BASIC PROPOSITION

Paul stated the basic reason for his defense in the middle of this paragraph (1Thess. 2:1-6). "On the contrary," he wrote, "we speak as men approved by God to be entrusted with the gospel. We are not trying to please men but God, who tests our hearts" (2:4).

There are two complementary aspects to this basic proposition.

They Were "Approved by God"

Paul made it clear that their authority for what they were teaching was from God (2:4). The Lord Himself was the divine Source of their message. Though all of the apostles were given special authority by Jesus Christ to preach the gospel, Paul in a special way received that message directly from God. Writing to the Galatians, he stated emphatically: "I did not receive it from any man, nor was I taught it; rather, I received it by revelation from Jesus Christ" (Gal. 1:12). Just so, Paul, Silas and Timothy were in Thessalonica on a special mission. They had been "approved by God."

They Were "Not Trying to Please Men"

This statement completes Paul's proposition (1 Thess. 2:4). The three missionaries did not come to Thessalonica to say things that would simply ingratiate themselves with people. They were not politicians seeking votes. They didn't soften their message to win a hearing and to be crowd pleasers. They simply delivered the gospel of Jesus Christ—that we are all sinners and need a Saviour; that Jesus Christ became our Saviour by dying for our sins on the cross and rising from the grave. Furthermore, Paul taught that if we put our faith in Jesus Christ and receive Him into our hearts and lives, we can be saved.

To the Jews, Paul demonstrated that Jesus Christ was the true Messiah promised in the Old Testament. To the unbelieving Gentiles, he proclaimed that there is only one true God. To worship Him they must receive Jesus Christ and turn from their idolatry. Obviously, this was not the most popular message that could be delivered in Thessalonica to either Jews or Gentiles. The facts are that many people rejected this message and eventually these missionaries had to leave Thessalonica because of persecution.

DIVINE AND HUMAN CONFIRMATION

Prior to the basic statement defending their ministry against criticism, Paul had already stated evidence that demonstrated their true reason for being in Thessalonica (2:1-3). The first reason points to a *divine factor* (2:1); the second gives the *human perspective* (2:2).

Their Ministry "Was Not a Failure"

After Paul and Silas and Timothy left Thessalonica, evidently false teachers and leaders tried to prove that the ministry of these three missionaries was a failure. Their words, of course, were contradicted by everything that had happened in Thessalonica. In fact, people all over Macedonia and Achaia and in every place were talking about the way in which the Thessalonians responded to the gospel—how they had "turned to God from idols to serve the living and true God" (1:9).

Some people who try to prove a point of view often ignore the facts. The most insidious approach is to lie and propagate false statements. Unfortunately, if a person repeats a false statement often enough, many people begin to believe it in spite of evidence to the contrary.

There seems to be something in all of us that causes us to want to believe negative statements rather than positive ones. Perhaps the reason relates to our own sense of insecurity or jealousy. For some of us it may be that our memories are just very short. Whatever the reasons, it happens and we must be on guard against this tendency. It is one of Satan's greatest tools. He knows it is possible to undermine a person's confidence in someone else with just a few seeds of negative criticism. Very quickly these seeds can sprout and grow into a whole field of doubt. This happened at times in Paul's ministry, often after he left a particular city.

They Continued Their Ministry in Spite of Severe Persecution

Here in verse 2 Paul used a human argument. Why would anyone risk his life to help others if his motives were to please men? Why go to prison—as Paul and Silas did in Philippi—if they were in that city for personal gain? Why allow yourself to be beaten and severely wounded in order to please yourself? This would be ridiculous and not sensible. It is totally contradictory to any kind of human logic.

This points, of course, to one of the strongest arguments to prove the validity of Christianity itself. If, for example, the Resurrection were a myth, as some people over the years have argued, why would the apostles be ready to die for that myth? In fact, most did give their lives for the message they taught.

This realization gives tremendous credence to the gospel message. And in this letter to the Thessalonians, Paul appeals to this reason for defending their ministry in Thessalonica. He wrote, "We had previously suffered and been insulted in Philippi . . . but with the help of our God we dared to tell you his gospel in spite of strong opposition" (2:2).

THEIR METHODS AND MOTIVATION

Throughout this passage (2:3,5-6), Paul also questions why they conducted themselves as they did and what the motives were behind their methods.

Their Appeal Did "Not Spring from Error"

Here in verse 3, Paul stated that they told the truth. They did not fabricate a story or perpetrate a myth. Since their motives were to glorify God, it follows they would not tell lies and untruths.

Since the beginning of Christianity, false teachers have arisen with false motives. They existed in Paul's day and they exist now. For example, Mary Baker Eddy, founder of the Christian Science movement, plagiarized extensively from several authors when she put together her volume *Science and Health*, the book that guides these people today. In fact, it can be demonstrated beyond a shadow of a doubt that she copied 33 pages verbatim and 100 pages in substance from Francis Leber, an authority on Hegel's philosophy of religion. Mrs. Eddy presented this material as her own—and started a new religion. At the same time, in her own writings she condemned plagiarism as being dishonest. It would seem her condemnation of this practice was a smoke screen to cover up her own sin.[1]

Their Appeal Did Not Spring from "Impure Motives"

In the second half of 1 Thessalonians 2:3, Paul refers to the charge that their motives were based on sexual immorality. This allegation must have been one of the most difficult criticisms to deal with emotionally—especially for a man who taught sexual purity as no other New Testament leader. It was understandable why this happened, because religious prostitution characterized many of the cults in the New Testament world. Understanding this context makes it clear that Paul was being accused of gross sexual immorality.

Again, this should not surprise us. There are many religious movements and many cults today that claim to be Christian and, on the surface, teach a very legalistic view of morality. However, the top leaders often have been exposed as engaging in the most blatant forms of sexual sin. The facts are that their legalistic system is only a smoke screen to cover up their own licentious behavior.

For a period of time there was a religious group operating in the southeastern part of the United States. On the surface it appeared to be evangelical theologically, evangelistic in its efforts in leading people to Christ and required a high level of morality and ethics of its followers—so much so it bordered on extreme legalism. After a period of time, the founder and leader of the movement was exposed as a blatant homosexual, taking advantage of new converts that he personally was supposed to be helping in their spiritual growth. More than anyone knows, this kind of smoke screen exists in religious cults to cover up immoral behavior. Unfortunately, this kind of behavior also exists in groups that preach and teach biblical truth.

They Did Not Use Any Form of Deception

The *New International Version* states: "Nor are we trying to trick you" (2:3). The word Paul used here actually signifies "catching fish with bait"—using some kind of means to trap them into some kind of religious system.

Here we're dealing with a delicate balance. Jesus stated that we are to be as wise as serpents and harmless as doves (see Matt. 10:16). He also taught His followers how to be "fishers of men" (see Matt. 4:19). But this in no way gives us license to be cunning and crafty and tricky.

Evangelistic tactics of some religious cults are designed with deceit in mind. Their initial presentations sound very biblical and harmless. But when a person becomes entangled in the religious system he or she is then taught false doctrine. At that point it is very difficult to discern truth from error, particularly when a form of brainwashing is a part of the system.

They Never Used Flattery

The Greek word which the *NIV* translates as "flattery" (1 Thess. 2:5) presents a concept difficult to explain. "Flattery," as we use the word in the English language, is not exactly what Paul had in mind. Leon Morris uses the word "cajolery" as meaning the use of acceptable speech with the purpose of lulling another into a false sense of security, so that one may obtain one's own ends.[2]

Let me try to illustrate this concept. Suppose someone approaches you with a proposal to invest some money in a special venture. All experienced and conservative-minded people who are in investments know this particular proposal is risky. But the person who is trying to sell you on the idea knows just what to say to put you at ease. He points out all of the positive possibilities. He cites those who have made it big—people you know at least by name. He tells you how much he's invested. His charts and graphs are impressive. The more he talks the more secure you feel. And before the evening is over, you've invested 90 percent of your savings in this venture, feeling excited about the great return you'll soon realize. Only time will tell if your excitement is justified.

Of course, *some* do make it in these situations. But the majority don't. In this case you end up losing everything— because someone sold you on a project with "flattery."

Paul is saying, "We did not promise you a rose garden when you became Christians. In fact, we told you ahead of time you would be persecuted and suffer. There were no hidden agendas in our message. We told you the truth, the whole truth and nothing but the truth. We offered you security in Christ, but not freedom from problems and difficulties."

They Did Not "Put on a Mask to Cover up Greed"

"God is our witness" to this fact, wrote Paul, emphasizing that they did not deceive these people by masking their motives (2:5). Evidently all three of these missionaries had been accused of having selfish reasons for being in Thessalonica—to see what they could get out of these people for personal gain. No doubt this criticism came from false teachers who knew their own hearts very well. It was not uncommon for religious leaders to take advantage of people financially.

Unfortunately, that is a common practice today among some religious hucksters. They know which buttons to push to open the pocketbook! Usually these people are not financially accountable to anyone. Their books are never opened.

One of the classic illustrations of this kind of behavior relates to the founder of the well-known religious group called Jehovah's Witnesses. The founder was Charles Russell and, through a well-planned strategy, he developed a large organization and controlled the entire financial holdings of the society. His deceptive methods for raising money are well documented. In fact, court case files expose Russell as a fraud![3] Jehovah's Witnesses today try to disprove these facts, but the facts cannot be denied. They are authenticated.

There were many people in the religious world of Paul's day with only one primary motive—material gain. Consequently, as the letter to the Thessalonians reveals, Paul sometimes bent over backward to make sure people could not accuse him of greed.

They Were Not Looking for Praise from Men

Paul had already defended his missionary team in this respect (1 Thess. 2:4). They were in Thessalonica to glorify God, not themselves. Had they been seeking self-glorification, there would certainly be better ways to obtain it. Why subject yourself to persecution, even endangering your life? To accuse Paul and his fellow missionaries of this kind of motivation is to completely ignore the facts. It had to be a projection of self-glorifying critics who were attempting to draw attention to themselves by accusing Paul of their very own sins.

HANDLING UNJUST CRITICISM

How should you and I handle unjust criticism? Paul demonstrates an unusual model for every twentieth-century Christian. First, of course, we should make sure it is *unjust* criticism. Perhaps there are valid reasons for the criticism. All of us at times make mistakes. Constructive criticism is helpful—although it is usually painful to receive.

But in the end if we're open and teachable, criticism produces maturity. The Scriptures state it well: "No discipline seems pleasant at the time, but painful. Later on, however, it produces a harvest of righteousness and peace for those who have been trained by it" (Heb. 12:11).

But what if the criticism is unjust, as it was with Paul and Silas and Timothy? Let's apply their model.

We Should Check Our Motives

Am I trying to please men or God? If we're pleasing God we'll obviously please others—particularly those who are committed to Jesus Christ. But remember that when God's will and ways are involved, Christians who are not living according to God's will (Paul called these people carnal Christians) often resist the truth. And if you are God's mouthpiece speaking the truth, they will often vent their resistance on you. And non-Christians may even be more critical.

At such times as this you and I must realize that pleasing God is more important than pleasing men. To be "approved by God" must always come first. And if indeed we know we are "approved by God," this can give us a tremendous sense of security, courage and inner peace in spite of unjust criticism.

Don't automatically expect criticism when you follow God. But when it comes, remember the words of Peter: "But in your hearts set apart Christ as Lord. Always be prepared to give an answer to everyone who asks you to give the reason for the hope that you have. But do this with gentleness and respect, keeping a clear conscience, so that those who speak maliciously against your good behavior in Christ may be ashamed of their slander" (1 Pet. 3:15-16).

We Should Check Our Methods

1. Do I always tell the truth?

Remember, it is easy to twist the truth—even when we don't intend to.

A caution: Remember that telling the truth does not always mean telling everything we know. This can be very unwise and even unfair. But in giving out *partial information,* we must be careful not to give *false impressions.*

2. Am I motivated by any kind of immoral or illegitimate desires?

Remember the words of Jeremiah: "The heart is deceitful above all things and beyond cure. Who can understand it?" (Jer. 17:9).

3. Am I using any form of deception to achieve a goal?

This concern, of course, is related to telling the truth. But it goes further. It involves our methodology—using ways and means to trick people into making decisions that ultimately will lead them down a path they otherwise might not take.

4. Do I use flattery; that is, a method that presents only the positive aspects of a decision and does not warn against possible problems that may also accompany the decision?

Note: Don't make up "negatives" just to have negatives. On the other hand, don't ignore the negatives if they are there.

5. Am I using methods that hide my real motives—such as greed or personal aggrandizement?

It's easy to use spiritual reasons to camouflage selfish desires. Here we must always be careful.

6. Do my methods serve to glorify God or myself?

It is not wrong to receive honor for a job well done. In fact, people who serve God well should and will be honored. But if our motives are to honor ourselves, we will not be honored by God.

We Should Let the Results of Our Efforts
Vindicate Our Motives and Methods

In essence, doing this allows God to defend us. As our divine attorney, He will do it right. It may not be according to our time schedule, but remember that we can trust Him.

This was Paul's most frequent approach. Though he did not hesitate to defend himself against false allegations and criticism, when all was said and done, it was the *results* of his ministry that proved to both Christians and non-Christians the purity of his motives and the correctness of his methods. Thus he wrote to the Thessalonians, "You know, brothers, that our visit to you was not a failure" (1 Thess. 2:1). People responded to the gospel. Lives were changed. God's Word flourished. And the whole world was talking about it.

During one period in my own personal ministry, I went through a time of severe criticism. Several individuals publicly accused me. It came as an incredible shock since it was made public to a large gathering of people. Ignoring the counsel and warnings of a number of mature spiritual leaders, they unveiled their list of criticisms anyway, violating clear biblical procedure for such matters.

Since I'm self-critical anyway, my first reactions were to introspect deeply. "Am I this kind of person?" I kept asking myself and others who knew me well. My wife and children kept reassuring me I was not that kind of person described by these criticisms. Other Christian leaders with whom I had worked for years also reassured me these criticisms were false and unjust. Frankly, if it had not been for these words of encouragement, I'm not sure what would have happened. I might have indeed given up the ministry.

In the midst of that crisis I felt the Lord leading me to do three important things.

First, He directed me to study the Scriptures as I never had before, seeking answers to my problem. The most encouraging thing I learned was that the criticism I had received was minor compared to what often happened to men like Paul and Silas and Timothy.

Second, He led me to learn what I could from these criticisms and to attempt to grow and mature through the process. As I developed more objectivity, I saw elements of truth in these criticisms, particularly because of my strong goal-oriented personality. Most important, I saw some naive and unwise decisions I had made that had opened the door for this circumstance to happen—particularly in my choice of leadership. I learned that my greatest strength was to trust people. However, I also learned that one of my greatest weaknesses was to trust people I shouldn't trust. I needed to be more discerning.

Third, God helped me to allow Him to set the record straight where the criticisms were unjust. With God's help, I determined not to defend myself.

I share this now, not to "defend myself," but to demonstrate that we can learn through crises. We can become better people. We can deepen our relationship with Jesus Christ. We can develop wisdom. We'll never become perfect, of course, and I'm sure I'll make some of the same mistakes again—at least to a certain degree. But, hopefully, I'll never be the same person again.

What about you?

Notes
1. Walter Martin, *The Kingdom of the Cults* (Minneapolis: Bethany Fellowship, Inc., 1965), pp. 112-113.
2. Leon Morris, *The Epistle of Paul to the Thessalonians* (Grand Rapids: Wm. B. Eerdmans Publishing Co., 1957), p. 46.
3. Martin, *The Kingdom of the Cults,* pp. 38-39.

5

A Powerful Communication Model

⁷As apostles of Christ we could have been a burden to you, but we were gentle among you, like a mother caring for her little children. ⁸We loved you so much that we were delighted to share with you not only the gospel of God but our lives as well, because you had become so dear to us. ⁹Surely you remember, brothers, our toil and hardship; we worked night and day in order not to be a burden to anyone while we preached the gospel of God to you.

¹⁰You are witnesses, and so is God, of how holy, righteous and blameless we were among you who believed. ¹¹For you know that we dealt with each of you as a father deals with his own children, ¹²encouraging, comforting and urging you to live lives worthy of God, who calls you into his kingdom and glory.

The very week I was writing this chapter, my wife and I drove our son to college to begin his freshman year. In one respect this was not an unusual experience. We had done the very same thing before with our two daughters. In another respect it was different. This was our youngest—and the last to leave the nest. In fact, we stayed at the college most of the day and attended a special seminar designed for parents who face the empty-nest syndrome.

Though we experienced some of the same emotional dynamics when each child left home to go to college, there were some unique aspects to these emotions this time around. As never before, we realized that our parenting responsibilities were virtually over. Questions flooded our minds. Did we do all we could to prepare these children-turning-adults for this moment? How will they handle the responsibility of this new independence? What will happen to the value system we've attempted to build into their lives? Will they stand firm against negative influences and peer pressures that may divert them from biblical principles and priorities?

And, of course, there is a whole other series of questions that relate to us as parents—especially when it is our last son or daughter to leave home. How will *we* handle the empty nest?

It hit my wife the moment we left the campus. She cried most of the way home—a very natural response for most mothers. Since my own emotions seem to operate on a time-delayed system, it hit me the next morning when I got up and realized my son wasn't in his room. In fact, I went and looked in his room twice. My first shock was to see how clean and neat it looked! On the serious side, the lump in my throat grew bigger as I realized that my son probably wouldn't be occupying that room again as a regular participant in our life as a family.

The question that accompanies this kind of experience for most of us as fathers is, How well did I fulfill my responsibility as a parent? I realized that in many respects my unique opportunities to influence my son in my role as his father were over. From this moment forward, he would walk into the future, building his life on the foundations that had already been laid.

The Apostle Paul, though he may never have had children of

his own, must have experienced all of these emotions every time he established a church and then left the people to fend for themselves. This comes through dramatically in Paul's letter to the Thessalonians, particularly in the passage we want to look at in this lesson (1 Thess. 2:7-12). In fact, Paul used the parental model to describe the ministry of Silas, Timothy and himself while in this city. Let's look more closely at what I've called "A Powerful Communication Model."

THE FIRST EXAMPLE: A NURSING MOTHER

When Paul and his fellow missionaries left the church at Thessalonica they were deeply concerned about the spiritual welfare of these new Christians (2:7-9). Consequently, they sent Timothy back to see how the Thessalonians were doing in their Christian lives (1 Thess. 3:1-5). Timothy's report was encouraging, even though false teachers had tried to discredit their ministry in Thessalonica. Paul wrote to the church presenting a subtle defense against these criticisms and then moved into a very positive stance regarding the kind of ministry they had with these people. To illustrate their mutual ministry among them Paul referred first of all to the relationship that should exist between a loving mother and her newborn child.

The Quality Demonstrated:
Unconditional Love

As you read this passage (vv. 7-9) describing the initial relationship the missionaries had with the Thessalonians, one quality emerges. Paul, Silas and Timothy demonstrated unconditional love toward them. *"We loved you so much,"* Paul wrote, "that we were delighted to share with you not only the gospel of God but our lives as well, because you had become so dear to us" (2:8).

No conditions! Unconditional love means just what it says— there are no conditions attached to that love. These men did not come to Thessalonica saying or implying, "We will love you *if* . . . . " In fact, Paul made it clear that, as apostles of Christ (that is, men sent by Christ), he and Timothy and Silas had a right to be supported by these people because they were ministering to them. Here Paul was definitely referring to their material support as missionaries, and he taught: "Do not muzzle an ox while it is treading out the grain" (1 Cor. 9:9; see Deut. 25:4). More specifically, "The worker deserves his wages" (1 Tim. 5:18).

In writing to these Thessalonian Christians, Paul was reminding them that as missionaries they could have used their God-ordained right and insisted on having their material needs met by the church. But they didn't. Rather, Paul wrote, "Surely you remember, brothers, our toil and hardship; we worked night and day in order not to be a burden to anyone while we preached the gospel of God to you" (1 Thess. 2:9).

Here we see how Paul's analogy becomes very meaningful. A newborn baby is not capable of responding in any way to a mother's care. Therefore, love toward that child, of necessity, is totally unconditional. And so Paul reminded these Thessalonians that the love he, Silas and Timothy demonstrated toward them was just as unconditional as the mother who cares for her newborn child. They expected nothing in return. Their motives were totally unselfish.

The Quality Illustrated:
The Mother-Child Relationship

Paul chose the mother-child relationship to illustrate their unconditional love toward these people. "As apostles of Christ," he wrote, "we could have been a burden to you, but we were gentle among you, like a mother caring for her little children" (1 Thess. 2:7).

Gentle care! The true test of their unconditional love was not only their self-sacrifice in giving up their rights. This is an outward manifestation that does not necessarily represent internal feelings.

Yet their love did reflect internal feelings—in gentleness, sensitivity and kindness toward these people. This is why Paul stated that their love was so deep for them that as missionaries they were willing to share "not only the gospel of God, but our lives as well" (1 Thess. 2:8). These men loved the Thessalonians from and with their very hearts and souls—with their total beings.

There is no more intimate and beautiful picture of unconditional love than that of a mother caring for her newborn and giving herself totally to this child. In such a manner, Paul stated, they treated the newborn Christians of Thessalonica. Peter used a similar analogy when he described new Christians as being "like newborn babies" who crave "pure spiritual milk" (1 Pet. 2:2). Paul and his co-workers gave milk to their newborns unconditionally so they would grow up in their salvation, strong and solid in the faith.

THE SECOND EXAMPLE: A NURTURING FATHER

The Quality Demonstrated: Consistent Care

The relationship these three missionaries had with the Thessalonian church was consistent, continual and caring. Consequently, under the nurturing of Paul, Silas and Timothy (1 Thess. 2:10-12), the people grew strong in their newfound faith.

The Quality Demonstrated: The Father-Child Relationship

As Paul reflected on the spiritual growth of these new Christians, he expanded his parental illustration of the relationship they enjoyed with the Thessalonians. "For you know," he wrote, "that we dealt with each of you as a *father* deals with his own children" (1 Thess. 2:11).

Again, note the specific ways this consistent care is illustrated.

An exemplary model

Paul first reminded these believers of the way in which they had demonstrated Christ among them: "You are witnesses, and so is God," he wrote, "of how *holy, righteous* and *blameless* we were among you who believed" (1 Thess. 2:10).

Paul, Silas and Timothy not only *told* these Christians how to live; they *showed* them how to live. They were a living demonstration of Christ's holy and righteous life. Earlier Paul had stated, "You know how we lived among you for your sake" (1:5). At this point in his letter he described in more detail how they lived. They modeled Jesus Christ.

A personal ministry

The father-child analogy used here by Paul has two important dimensions. As we've just seen, modeling Christ is foundational. Dealing with each person as an individual is the second. No child in any family is identical to the others in terms of personal needs. We must not treat them all alike. This, Paul implied, is part of a father's parenting responsibility.

As parents deal individually with their own children, we must personalize our ministry to others. Just so, Paul stated as he wrote to these believers, "We dealt with each of you as a father deals with his own children" (1 Thess. 2:11).

How this happened we do not know. Perhaps these three men divided up the church amongst themselves and made sure that each person was ministered to by one of them. Perhaps they selected other mature and growing Christians in the group to help them carry out this process. But whatever the method, it is clear that their ministry was individualized. They encouraged each one, comforted each one, and urged each one "to live lives worthy of God" (2:12).

APPLYING THIS COMMUNICATION MODEL TODAY

Paul, Silas and Timothy demonstrated two very obvious areas in which we can apply the principles of communication demonstrated by Paul, Silas and Timothy. The first involves the church itself. These New Testament missionaries illustrate for us principles of communication for planting and building mature churches.

The second area of application involves the family. What Paul tells us about parental function is to a great extent even more foundational, since this is the social unit Paul, Silas, and Timothy used as their model for a ministry at the local church level.

How can we apply these principles in both areas?

In the Church

1. Effective communication must be built on unconditional love.

This means we must be willing to give to others without expecting something in return. True, we all have reciprocal responsibilities. People who become receivers and takers only are not mature in Jesus Christ. Those who let others minister to them without ministering in return are living selfish Christian lives.

Yet mature Christians must realize that many people in the Church of Jesus Christ are still infants and babes in Christ. They have not yet learned to minister to others. This is why the Thessalonians needed models when they first became Christians. And it worked, for Paul wrote, "You became imitators of us and of the Lord" (1 Thess. 1:6).

2. Effective communication must be sensitive.

Paul made this point very clear in his second letter to Timothy, who often faced the difficult challenge of helping new believers grow in their faith. In the process, he met people who were resistant to spiritual growth and some who openly opposed his efforts.

Thus Paul wrote to his co-worker: "And the Lord's servant must not quarrel; instead, he must be kind to everyone, able to teach, not resentful. Those who oppose him he must *gently instruct,* in the hope that God will grant them repentance leading them to a knowledge of the truth, and that they will come to their senses and escape from the trap of the devil, who has taken them captive to do his will" (2 Tim. 2:24-26).

Interestingly, this is the only other time the Greek word translated "gentle" in Paul's mother-child analogy in 1 Thessalonians 2:7 is used in the New Testament. Also, it is only the second time Paul used the basic concept "able to teach." The first time was when he listed the qualifications for elders in 1 Timothy 3:2. This, of course, shows the clear relationship between gentleness and effective communication.

Paul's instruction to Timothy has unusual implications. Let me illustrate what he means in relation to both his mother-child analogy in Thessalonians and his instructions to Timothy.

One of the elders in our church is the chief operating officer of a large savings and loan organization. One Saturday morning Mike and his wife Sharon were seated in their home. Hearing some activity going on outside the house, Sharon went to the window, pulled the drapes and looked out. A large bus had pulled up in front of their home. As people got off the bus, they were handed placards and began to march up and down the sidewalk in front of the house.

Shortly, there was a knock at the door. Standing there was one of the leaders of the group with a written document. In essence, the document accused the savings and loan organization of being unfair to minorities. So a group of minority people had arrived by bus and were picketing Mike and Sharon's home. Since Mike was the chief operating officer of this loan organization, his home was targeted for this activity.

The gentleman who had knocked on the door asked Mike to sign a confession that the organization was indeed guilty of this charge. Incidentally, standing beside this gentleman was a man with a camera, ready to take a picture of what they predicted would be resistance—perhaps an argument or a slammed door.

Mike's response dramatically impacted my own life. Rather than discuss the document with the leader of the group, he invited him to come into his home and discuss the issue. In fact, he suggested that he go back to the group that was marching up and down on the sidewalk in front of his home and invite everyone to join them in the family room for coffee.

Needless to say, the demonstrators were nonplussed. However, after a brief huddle, they all filed into Mike's home, sat in the family room and drank coffee while Mike shared with them his own concerns about minorities in the city of Dallas. He shared his involvements on various community committees and with various groups in attempting to be fair and equitable. In essence, he was sharing with them the truth about his leadership in his organization. And in the process, Mike was able to shift into his personal testimony and share how he had come to know Jesus Christ and how it had changed his life and even intensified his desire to manage his business affairs according to Christian principles.

In that context Mike had a captive audience. In fact, he began to get affirmations and even a few "amens" from the group. To make a long story short, eventually the dissenters got up, thanked Mike and Sharon for their hospitality, walked out the door, got on the bus and left without creating any further disturbance.

As I heard Mike share this experience, my mind went immediately to this passage of Scripture Paul shared with Timothy. Under those same conditions my initial reactions would be to quarrel or argue—particularly since the charges were false. But Paul told Timothy that "the Lord's servant must not quarrel." Instead, he is to "be kind to everyone."

We are not to be resentful. We are to "gently instruct" those people who oppose us. This, Paul says, will make us "able to teach" (2 Tim. 2:24-25). In other words, Paul is saying that this kind of instruction opens the hearts of people to listen to the truth. Thus, effective communication in the church must be straightforward, but sensitive. Most people—not all—respond to this kind of approach.

3. Effective communication must be built on modeling.

In essence, Paul is telling us that Christians must first of all practice what they preach. We will never win a hearing by being inconsistent in our life-style. And those of us in church leadership must take this principle very seriously. No one, of course, is perfect. But there is a level of consistency that is attainable in Christ and expected by those we minister to.

4. Effective communication must be personal.

This is the most difficult principle to practice consistently, particularly as a church grows numerically. This is why in our own church we attempt to involve our people in small groups led by lay pastors. This is also why we try to add to our pastoral staff as the church grows, so that we can attempt to keep up with people's needs.

Even at that, it is easy to become impersonal. The whole

Body must be committed to one-on-one communication. This is not a task only for the leadership. And it is certainly important for members of the Body to communicate needs people have that might go unnoticed by church leaders.

We must remember, however, that some people will not commit themselves to a group where they can be ministered to. It is often these people who become lost in the system. At some point they must take responsibility for becoming part of the ministry so that their needs can be met, too.

In the Home

These principles, as stated earlier, actually grow out of Paul's view of parent-child relationships in the family. Thus we need to ask ourselves as parents some very pointed and practical questions:

1. To what extent is our communication built on unconditional love?
2. To what extent is our communication sensitive?
3. To what extent is our communication built on modeling Christian truths?
4. To what extent is our communication personal, involving *each* child?

As I reflect on these questions, particularly as a father, I am well aware that my unique opportunities in the home are now gone. And, being a pastor, I am also aware that over the years I have often gotten caught between the personal needs of people in the larger church family and the personal needs of my own children. Unfortunately, I have at times made people's needs in the church a priority over my children's needs.

Do understand that I'm not blaming the people in the churches I've pastored. The choice has always been mine. There are times I've just not made correct decisions. One reason is that I tend—as we all do—to take those closest to me for granted. "They'll understand," I rationalize.

To the credit of my own children—now grown—they have

understood beyond what should have been expected. They've been on my team. And I must hasten to add that they have understood many times because of my wife's faithful support. Often she interpreted to them the demands on my time which made it easier for them to accept my decisions to be with others rather than with them.

But I must also share that I often wish I had my fathering experience to do over again. If so, I would attempt to make one important change. *Each one* of my children would get more of my time and attention.

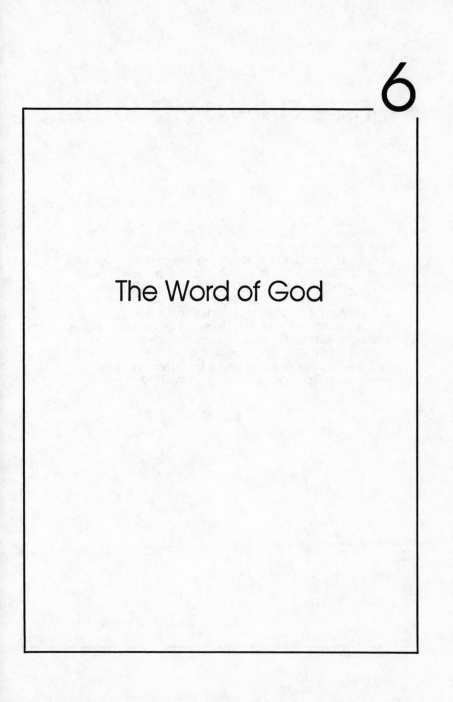

6

The Word of God

¹³And we also thank God continually because, when you received the word of God, which you heard from us, you accepted it not as the word of men, but as it actually is, the word of God, which is at work in you who believe. ¹⁴For you, brothers, became imitators of God's churches in Judea, which are in Christ Jesus: You suffered from your own countrymen the same things those churches suffered from the Jews, ¹⁵who killed the Lord Jesus and the prophets and also drove us out. They displease God and are hostile to all men ¹⁶in their effort to keep us from speaking to the Gentiles so that they may be saved. In this way they always heap up their sins to the limit. The wrath of God has come upon them at last.

Chuck Swindoll once reported that during his days in New England he heard of a teacher named Thayer S. Warshaw, who quizzed a group of college-bound high school juniors and seniors on the Bible. The quiz preceded a "Bible as Literature" class he planned to teach at Newton (Mass.) High School, generally considered one of the best public schools in the nation. Among the most outstanding findings he got in his replies from students were:

"Jezebel was Ahab's donkey."

"Sodom and Gomorrah were lovers."

"The four horsemen in the Book of Revelation appeared on the Acropolis."

"The New Testament Gospels were written by Matthew, Mark, Luther and John."

"Eve was created from an apple."

"Jesus was baptized by Moses."

"Epistles are the wives of apostles."

But the answer that took the cake was given by a fellow who ranked academically in the top 5 percent of the graduating class.

The question: What was Golgotha?

The answer: Golgotha was the name of the giant who slew the apostle David.[1]

The Bible is the most important book in the world. Its truth will never pass away but will endure forever (Matt. 24:35). It has dramatically influenced some of the most outstanding leaders in world history. Martin Luther once stated, "The Bible is alive, it speaks to me; it has feet, it runs after me; it has hands, it lays hold of me."

Abraham Lincoln testified, "I believe the Bible is the best gift that God has ever given to man. All the good from the Saviour of the world is communicated to us through this Book. I have been driven many times to my knees by the overwhelming conviction that I had nowhere else to go."[2]

Charles Haddon Spurgeon, a great Bible student and teacher, once stated, "A Bible which is falling apart usually belongs to someone who is not."[3]

When all is said and done, it is God's Word that is basic to any success we may have in seeing people come to Jesus Christ and grow in Jesus Christ. Man's philosophy and wisdom may bring change—even positive change—to people's lives, but it's only God's Word that endures and causes people to persist in doing the will of God.

Paul knew this to be true and testified to that fact in his letter to the Thessalonian Christians. Thus he wrote, "And we also thank God continually because, when you received the word of God, which you heard from us, you accepted it not as the word of men, but as it actually is, the *word of God*" (1 Thess. 2:13).

THE WORD—ITS SOURCE

Paul and his two missionary companions, Silas and Timothy, had one primary message when they came into a pagan city. That message was the Word of God. And when Paul wrote to the Thessalonians he expressed thankfulness that the Thessalonians received their message and accepted it—not as the word of men—but as it really is—God's eternal Word.

There were many false teachers in the New Testament world, and multitudes of people were following their human teachings. This is why Paul warned the Colossian Christians, "See to it that no one takes you captive through *hollow* and *deceptive philosophy,* which depends on *human tradition* and the *basic principles of this world* rather than on Christ" (Col. 2:8).

A Supernatural Process

There are many people today who question the authority of Scripture. They do not believe it is God's Word. Space prohibits developing the multitude of reasons why we should accept the Bible as God's inspired Word. If you are struggling with that question, I'd suggest you read *Evidence That Demands a Verdict* by Josh McDowell. McDowell points out that the Bible has been—

• written over a 1600-year span
• written over 60 generations
• written by 40 + authors from every walk of life, including

kings, peasants, philosophers, fishermen, poets, statesmen, scholars, etc.

- written in different places
- written at different times
- written during different moods
- written on three continents
- written in three languages

"Biblical authors spoke on hundreds of controversial subjects with harmony and continuity from Genesis to Revelation," writes McDowell. "There is one unfolding story: 'God's redemption of man.'"[4]

Most people who do not believe the Bible are people who have not studied the Bible carefully—its origins, its content and how it compares with other religious literature. For example, Professor M. Montiero-Williams, former Boden professor of Sanskrit, spent 42 years studying Eastern books and, in comparing them with the Bible, said: "Pile them, if you will, on the left side of your study table; but place your own Holy Bible on the right side—all by itself, all alone—and with a wide gap between them. For, . . . there is a gulf between it and the so-called sacred books of the East which severs the one from the other, utterly, hopelessly, and forever . . . a veritable gulf which cannot be bridged over by any science of religious thought."[5]

When I was working on my doctorate at New York University I was required to take a course in "Comparative Religions." It was one of the most challenging courses I've taken in my educational career. It gave me the opportunity to read and study the Koran—the sacred writings from the Muslim religion. I also studied the writings that form the basis for Hinduism, Buddhism and other Eastern religions. The more I studied, the more convinced I became that there can be no significant comparison of these books with the Bible, even in terms of literary quality. It was a very faith-strengthening experience.

A Supracultural Product

Let me add a couple of additional thoughts that have strengthened my faith in the Bible as being the Word of God.

First, the more I study the Scriptures and the more I teach them, the more assured I am that the Bible is, indeed, God's inspired Word. No human being could write with the depth, perception and uniqueness of the writers of Scripture without supernatural guidance and assistance.

I am gripped again and again by the way in which writers of Scripture have written so as to leave us with truth that transcends time and is applicable to every culture of the world. One aspect of this reality is the way in which no writer of Scripture has locked us into cultural form and structure. Rather, they give us basic functions and principles that can be applied at any moment in history and in any place in the world.

How easy it would have been for the authors of Scripture to lock us into the cultures of the New Testament world. Had they done so, Christianity would have become just another Eastern religion. It would have been so related to its cultural birthplace that it would have either died out or fixated in one geographical area of the world. Rather, its supracultural dimensions has allowed it to spread to every part of the world. In that sense, Christianity is uniquely different from any other major world religion. Most cannot survive out of their cultures—unless they change their theology. Conversely, Christianity *has* survived and grown and spread to a multitude of cultures without changing its theology. Only truth inspired by God could create this kind of worldwide influence.

Since that day when the Thessalonians accepted the Word of God, people all over the world have responded in the same way. Furthermore, when it is received and accepted, the Word of God does its work in the hearts of people, just as it did in Thessalonica. Thus Paul wrote, "You accepted it not as the word of men, but as it actually is, the word of God, *which is at work in you who believe*" (1 Thess. 2:13).

THE WORD—ITS WORK

Note that Paul used two words to describe the Thessalonians' response to their message. They first "*received* the word of God" and secondly, they "*accepted* it" (2:13). To "receive" the message was more of an *external* response. They listened and evaluated the message. But to "accept" the Word of God represents an *internal* response. The same Greek word was used in the New Testament to welcome a guest into your home.

Today many people receive the Word of God. They don't even resist it. In reality they are passive. They do not accept it in the sense of welcoming the truth into their hearts and lives and acting on that truth. Many of the Thessalonians took both steps. They listened *and* responded!

What happens to Christians who truly accept the Word of God? *First,* they are born again (Jas. 1:18). *Second,* they will experience spiritual growth, just as an infant grows on mother's milk, following through on Paul's "nursing mother" analogy (1 Thess. 2:7). This is why Peter also exhorted, "Like newborn babies, crave pure spiritual milk, so that by it you may grow up in your salvation, now that you have tasted that the Lord is good" (1 Pet. 2:2-3).

In writing to Timothy, Paul outlined very specifically what happens to a Christian who both receives and accepts the Word of God. Timothy had been taught the Holy Scriptures from childhood. And it is the Holy Scriptures, wrote Paul, "which are able to make you wise for salvation through faith in Christ Jesus" (2 Tim. 3:15). Again, this is step 1 in accepting the Word of God. The basic and most important message of Scripture is that Jesus Christ is the Saviour of the world and that, in receiving Him as personal Saviour, we become children of God.

In this letter to Timothy, Paul also emphasizes step 2— allowing the Word of God to do its work in our hearts as believers. Thus Paul continued, "All Scripture is God-breathed and is useful for *teaching, rebuking, correcting* and *training* in righteousness, so that the man of God may be thoroughly equipped for every good work" (2 Tim. 3:16-17).

Here Paul affirmed the Source of his message—God Himself. The Holy Scriptures are inspired by God. The words of the Bible represent the very "breath of God." He is the divine author.

Paul then outlines what happens to a believer who accepts this "God-breathed" message. It teaches us; it rebukes us; it corrects us; in short, it trains us "in righteousness" and equips us to do God's will and work in this world (3:16-17).

I received a beautiful letter from a member of our own church one day that was a real encouragement to me and verifies what Paul wrote to Timothy:

> When we first came to the church, we were not walking in the Word and did not understand how to apply the Bible to our lives. With the years, as we've learned more and more and grown in faith through trusting Him, we've seen how the Lord has truly blessed us and we're so grateful.
>
> Also, we've enjoyed the Bible verses you put at the end of the message outlines. They've really helped us be consistent in Bible study and thus grow.

It's letters like this that cause a pastor to keep his eyes fixed on the goal of teaching the Bible clearly and carefully week after week. It also verifies the reality of the Scriptures themselves; for, indeed, God says that the Word of God is the basic means for spiritual growth and maturity.

THE WORD—ITS RESULTS

Prior to this paragraph (1 Thess. 2:14-16) in his letter, Paul had already described the positive results of the Word of God in the lives of these believers. They "turned to God from idols to serve the living and true God." Furthermore, they were looking forward to the second coming of Jesus Christ (1 Thess. 1:9-10). Their faith in God was so dynamic that it was being talked about not only in the immediate community but all over the New Testament world.

But something else happened when they accepted the Word of God. They were persecuted. This, however, was not a surprise because Paul had warned them it would come (1 Thess. 3:4). In this sense they "became imitators of God's churches in Judea" (2:14). Paul is referring to the fact that many Jews turned to Christ, and as a result they were persecuted by their fellow Jews. Paul, of course, knew all about this firsthand because he was the chief persecutor before he became a Christian.

Paul seems to be saying that those Jews who lived in their area did the same thing to the Thessalonian church that they did to the churches in Judea. Luke records that many of them "were jealous." They were the ones who "rounded up some bad characters from the marketplace, formed a mob and started a riot in the city" (Acts 17:5). It was the Jews of Thessalonica who initiated the persecution and eventually drove these missionaries out of Thessalonica.

Furthermore, Luke also records that "when the Jews in Thessalonica learned that Paul was preaching the word of God at Berea, they went there too, agitating the crowds and stirring them up" (Acts 17:13).

The primary source of persecution, then, appears to be the Jews. Paul indicted them with these words: "They displease God and are hostile to all men in their effort to keep us from speaking to the Gentiles so that they may be saved. In this way they always heap up their sins to the limit. The wrath of God has come upon them at last" (1 Thess. 2:15-16).

Here Paul was referring to the judgment that would eventually come upon those Jews who continue to reject their Messiah and, in the process, try to keep others from hearing about Jesus Christ (see Rom. 9:1-33). The setting is uniquely New Testament, for in the early days of Christianity many Jews— particularly the leaders—were extremely hostile to the message of Christianity. And to this very day, the whole nation is suffering the results of this rejection of Jesus Christ, just as it was prophesied in the Old Testament. Here Paul, the former persecutor of Christians, was affirming the judgment God would bring upon Israel for their hardness of heart.

But what happens generally to believers who receive the Word, accept it in their hearts and allow it to work in their lives? Paul made this clear in his letter to Timothy. After outlining the way in which the Holy Scriptures work in a person's heart who receives and accepts this truth by "teaching, rebuking, correcting and training in righteousness," Paul states the result: "So that the man of God may be thoroughly equipped for every good work" (2 Tim. 3:17).

We'll Become Mature in Christ

In 2 Timothy 3:17, Paul used the phrase "man of God" because he was speaking to Timothy. This term, however, can be generalized to all Christians. God's will for our lives is that we become men and women of God! It is the Word of God that is foundational to producing this maturity.

During the time I was on the faculty at Moody Bible Institute in Chicago, I was privileged to get to know MBI's then president, Dr. William Culbertson, quite well. In fact, I got to know him best while playing volleyball. A number of staff and faculty men got together at noon several times a week to play. We played together for more than 10 years, and when we played in competition, we lost very few games, primarily because of our years of practice and experience. Those were fun days!

Dr. Culbertson and I had lockers next to each other, so we had a lot of interaction and communication before, during and after games. He was one of the best setup men I've ever worked with and, if you've watched the Olympics, you know how important setups are in enabling a player to spike the ball .

Dr. Culbertson was many years my senior and in many respects the man I looked up to as my spiritual model—whether I was listening to him in faculty meetings and Monday morning chapel or playing by his side on the volleyball court. He deeply impressed me as a man of the Word. He loved the Bible and he loved to teach it to others. And he lived out in his daily life what he was learning and teaching from God's Word.

Don't misunderstand. He wasn't perfect by any means. In fact, he was a fierce competitor on the volleyball court and sometimes allowed his enthusiasm for winning to go a little too far. But he was also quick to correct any wrong attitudes and actions.

When Dr. Culbertson died, Warren Wiersbe was chosen to write the story of his life. When searching for a title he finally decided on *William Culbertson—A Man of God!* This title describes his life. He believed with all his heart that "all Scripture is God-breathed" and is "useful for teaching, rebuking, correcting and training in righteousness." And when the Word of

God is allowed to do this kind of work in our lives, it produces a man of God—a woman of God!

We'll Be Equipped for Every Good Work

All Christians face a variety of tasks and challenges! And there are thousands of university programs designed to equip us to perform these tasks and meet these challenges. But there is no course more important to prepare us to face life—in any situation—than the Word of God. It is foundational to all we do.

Don't misunderstand. I'm not talking specifically about being a minister or a missionary. Obviously, these Christian vocations demand in a special way an experiential knowledge of the Word of God. Tragically, there are many people who try to perform these professions without a knowledge of the Scriptures. In fact, some don't even believe the Bible *is* the Word of God.

But I'm referring to *every* vocation in life. An experiential knowledge of Scripture is still foundational in equipping all of us to do our jobs effectively (2 Tim. 3:17). It will give us strength to face the demands that are placed upon us. It will give us moral courage to live above the sin that surrounds us. It will give us ethical fiber in our souls never to compromise the laws of God. The Word of God will equip you and me for *every good work!*

THE WORD OF GOD AND YOU

What about you? Are you allowing the Word of God to do the work of God in your life? Consider these questions:

1. Have you really accepted the Word of God?

That is, are you obeying it? Do you allow it to guide you and direct you in all you do? Or have you just received it—listened to it, affirmed it—but not acted on it, allowing it to really direct the course of your life?

On May 21, 1941 the "unsinkable" Nazi battleship, the *Bismarck,* was sighted by the Allies in the North Atlantic. Immediately, planes and ships from the Royal British Navy sped to the scene. As the *Bismarck* headed toward the German-controlled French coast, to the astonishment of all, the massive battleship suddenly swung around and reentered the area where the British ships were massed in greatest strength. At the same time, she began to steer an erratic zigzag course. A torpedo had damaged her rudder after all. Consequently, the "unsinkable" *Bismarck* was sunk.

As Christians, our rudder is the Bible, without which we will become unguided in our Christian walk.

2. Are you reading and studying the Word on your own?

As twentieth-century Christians, we have a unique advantage over first-century believers. First, we have it *all*—the whole Bible. Remember, the only pieces of New Testament literature the Thessalonians may have seen were the two letters Paul sent them. In fact, some of the Thessalonian Christians evidently died before they even received the first letter (1 Thess. 4:13-18). Some of them probably never experienced seeing or hearing one piece of New Testament literature—and maybe very little Old Testament literature, since many were not Jews.

It would be many centuries before the New Testament would be published in one volume. And it would be many centuries more before the average person could afford to purchase the Bible in his own language. We *are* a privileged people. Are you using that privilege to study the Word of God in order to equip yourself for the work that God has for you to do in this world?

Notes
1. Paul Lee Tan, *Signs of the Time* (Rockville, Md.: Assurance Publications, 1979).
2. Ibid.
3. Ibid.
4. Taken from EVIDENCE THAT DEMANDS A VERDICT by Josh McDowell, © Campus Crusade for Christ, 1972, 1979. Published by Here's Life Publishers. Used by permission.

7

Paul's Emotional Experiences

1 THESSALONIANS 2:17-3:13

¹⁷But, brothers, when we were torn away from you for a short time (in person, not in thought), out of our intense longing we made every effort to see you. ¹⁸For we wanted to come to you—certainly I, Paul, did, again and again—but Satan stopped us. ¹⁹For what is our hope, our joy, or the crown in which we will glory in the presence of our Lord Jesus Christ when he comes? Is it not you? ²⁰Indeed, you are our glory and joy.

^{3:1}So when we could stand it no longer, we thought it best to be left by ourselves in Athens. ²We sent Timothy, who is our brother and God's fellow worker in spreading the gospel of Christ, to strengthen and encourage you in your faith, ³so that no one would be unsettled by these trials. You know quite well that we were destined for them. ⁴In fact, when we were with you, we kept telling you that we would be persecuted. And it turned out that way, as you well know. ⁵For this reason, when I could stand it no longer, I sent to find out about your faith. I was afraid that in some way the tempter might have tempted you and our efforts might have been useless.

⁶But Timothy has just now come to us from you and has brought good news about your faith and love. He has told us that you always have pleasant memories of us and that you long to see us, just as we also long to see you. ⁷Therefore, brothers, in all our distress and persecution we were encouraged about you because of your faith. ⁸For now we really live, since you are standing firm in the Lord. ⁹How can we thank God enough for you in return for all the joy we have in the presence of our God because of you? ¹⁰Night and day we pray most earnestly that we may see you again and supply what is lacking in your faith.

¹¹Now may our God and Father himself and our Lord Jesus clear the way for us to come to you. ¹²May the Lord make your love increase and overflow for each other and for everyone else, just as ours does for you. ¹³May he strengthen your hearts so that you may be blameless and holy in the presence of our God and Father when our Lord Jesus comes with all his holy ones.

In this section of Paul's letter (1 Thess. 2:17—3:13), he opened his heart and revealed his humanness—his emotions. It is true that Paul used the plural pronouns "we" and "our" and "us," throughout this section, but the focus is clearly on his personal feelings and emotional reactions, both in a positive and negative sense.[1]

Here we see Paul, the man, the human being. This is encouraging since we tend to idealize people of his stature, falsely concluding that they somehow lived above the emotional struggles and difficulties of life. Not so! And Paul's personal openness at this point in his letter demonstrates his internal struggles. More important than his emotions per se, however, are the actions he took when he experienced these emotions.

PAUL'S NEGATIVE FEELINGS

1. Anxiety (2:17; 3:1). This particular emotion is described more functionally than specifically in this passage. However, it is clearly implied in what Paul wrote. He had an "intense longing" to see them (2:17). In fact, his anxiety became so intense, he had no choice but to do something about it. "So," he wrote, *"when we could stand it no longer,* we thought it best to be left by ourselves in Athens" (3:1).

This is a very emotional statement. It really means that Paul's anxiety and deep concern for these people were becoming intolerable. Also, *kataleipo,* the word Paul used to describe being "left" alone in Athens, implies a feeling of being abandoned. Mark used the word to describe the man who dies and leaves his wife (Mark 12:19). It was extremely traumatic for Paul to be left alone. He said good-bye to Timothy with a deep sense of privation.

2. Fear (1 Thess. 3:5). In his anxiety, Paul also expresses feelings of fear. The *NIV* reads: "I was *afraid* that in some way the tempter might have tempted you and our efforts might have been useless." Though the word "fear" is not used in the original language of the New Testament, it is certainly implied in Paul's statement. Furthermore, anyone who can identify with Paul's concern about these people can also identify with his emotions.

Fear is a more specific manifestation of anxiety and can be very intense and difficult to handle. For most human beings, it's the kind of emotion that can lead to sleepless nights.

3. *Distress* (3:7). Paul made reference to a third negative emotion in verse 7. The context is persecution and affliction. The feeling is distress.

Again, we have a more specific description of anxiety. Heretofore, Paul was describing his negative emotions regarding the status of the Christians in Thessalonica. Here he was referring to the inward anxiety he was experiencing because of those who were attacking his ministry. More specifically, they were attacking him personally.

Much of the persecution Paul faced involved his physical well-being, which he described graphically when he wrote to the Corinthians (2 Cor. 11:24-27):

- Five times I received from the Jews the 40 lashes minus one.
- Three times I was beaten with rods.
- Once I was stoned.
- Three times I was shipwrecked.
- I spent a night and a day in the open sea.
- I have been constantly on the move.
- I have been in danger from rivers, from bandits, from my own countrymen, from Gentiles, in the city, in the country, at sea and from false brothers.
- I have labored and toiled and have often gone without sleep.
- I have known hunger and thirst and have often gone without food.
- I have been cold and naked.

Paul culminates this very graphic paragraph by referring to that which was creating his greatest anxiety regarding the Thessalonians. "Besides everything else," he concluded, "I face daily the pressure of my concern for all the churches" (2 Cor. 11:28).

Paul's Reasons

To understand more fully what Paul was actually feeling, we

need to look more carefully at the reasons for Paul's anxiety. He stated at least three.

1. Paul was "torn away" from the Thessalonians (1 Thess. 2:17).

This reference takes us back to those difficult days described in Acts 17 when the Jews became jealous and "formed a mob and started a riot in the city" (Acts 17:5). The persecution became so intense that Paul and Silas had to flee for their lives.

The words to be "torn away" help explain the kind of anxiety Paul felt when he left Thessalonica, but also the kind of anxiety he felt when he could not go back and see them. The expression Paul used to describe this experience literally means "to be orphaned."

Again, we see a correlation with the father and mother illustration Paul used earlier in the letter. These people were his "children" in Christ. He had cared for them like a nursing mother and had encouraged and comforted them like a caring and nurturing father (1 Thess. 2:7,11).

Many of us have observed on film some of the horrible scenes from World War II when Jewish fathers and mothers were "torn away" from their children and sent off to different locations, sometimes never to see each other again. Imagine the inner pain! In some respects Paul was so emotionally involved with the people he had led to Christ that he suffered incredible anxiety when he had to leave them because of the persecution just described in Acts 17. Under these conditions, he did not know whether or not he would ever see these people again. Furthermore, he was concerned about what would happen to them, both physically and spiritually.

2. Paul had tried to see them again, but Satan had thwarted his efforts (1 Thess. 2:18).

Paul's struggles with anxiety were caused by more than environmental barriers that kept him from going back to Thessalonica. He was also in a battle with Satan himself. Thus he wrote, "For we wanted to come to you—certainly I, Paul, did, again and again—but Satan stopped us" (2:18).

Notice that Paul had endeavored to return to Thessalonica on several occasions.[2] But each time he was blocked by the greatest evil personality in the universe—the devil himself.

Paul does not tell us specifically how this happened. Certainly, Satan works in a multitude of different ways to thwart God's work. However, here it appears that Satan was in some way directly involved in these circumstances.

It is possible that Paul was referring to the way Satan was using those who opposed the apostle's ministry. If this is true, we can more clearly understand the dynamics involved. Certainly, there is no question that the Jews, who openly and violently opposed Jesus Christ, were controlled by Satan. This is why Jesus so bluntly stated, "You belong to your father, the devil, and you want to carry out your father's desires" (John 8:44).

3. Paul was afraid Satan may have led these new believers astray (1 Thess. 3:5).

This concern is one of the primary reasons Paul was so anxious and desirous to return to Thessalonica. "I was afraid," he wrote, "that in some way the tempter might have tempted you and our efforts might have been useless" (3:5).

Paul evidently felt very good about the Thessalonians' initial response to his ministry. But it wasn't until he received a positive report from Timothy that he was absolutely sure that these people were truly converted to Jesus Christ. How had they stood up to the persecution once he and his fellow missionaries had left? Had the Word of God really taken root in their lives? Were they truly born again? Were they growing in faith and hope and love?

These and many other questions no doubt flooded Paul's mind. And they created a great deal of anxiety for this sensitive and tenderhearted man.

Paul's Actions

Paul's actions in response to what he was feeling is more important than the emotions themselves. Paul's anxiety over these unanswered questions motivated him to action. He decided to stay in Athens and to send Timothy back to Thessalonica. This in itself was a very difficult decision. He wanted to go personally, but probably knew that his presence in Thessalonica might accentuate the persecution against the believers there—giving Satan the opportunity he needed to accomplish his insidious goals. Since Timothy's profile was much lower than his, he made a decision to send his missionary companion.

Note the two reasons Paul states as to why he took this action.

1. He sent Timothy to find out about the Thessalonians' faith (3:5).

Though this reason appears second in this section of the letter, it is the primary reason. Thus Paul wrote, "For this reason, when I could stand it no longer, I send to find out about your faith" (3:5). Paul wanted to know if it was real.

2. He sent Timothy to strengthen and encourage them in their faith (3:2).

Though Paul was concerned whether these people had become true believers, he felt that evidence indicated they were members of the family of God. But Paul also knew what persecution could do to "new Christians." He knew that they could be sidetracked from the will of God and waver in their faith. Thus he wrote, "We sent Timothy . . . to strengthen and encourage you in your faith so that no one would be unsettled by these trials" (3:2-3).

PAUL'S POSITIVE FEELINGS

Paul also described the positive emotions he felt, resulting from the actions he took in sending Timothy to Thessalonica. And we can isolate both the *reasons* for these emotions and the *actions* Paul took once he received a positive report from Timothy.

Encouragement (3:7). Paul used the word "encouraged" to describe his emotional reaction to Timothy's positive report. This, of course, is predictable and all of us can identify with the good feelings that are associated with this word.

I remember a time when I became deeply concerned about a dear Christian friend of mine who lived in another city. I had counseled her through some very difficult times in her emotional life as well as in her business career. Then, suddenly, I couldn't seem to make contact with her. She didn't answer my letters or my phone calls.

My first concern was that I might have said or done something that had offended her. I was also concerned that she might no longer feel the same sense of relationship with my wife and me. Then again, I was concerned that something may have sidetracked her spiritually and she was now avoiding me.

Rather than back off, I decided to step up my efforts at communication and finally made contact. She *had* gone through a difficult period in her life that was combined with a very hectic and pressurized schedule.

Once I discovered why our communication seemed to have broken down I felt relief and encouragement. More important, I was encouraged that she had worked through an experience that could have been disastrous had she made a bad decision.

I'm sure my encouragement was minor compared to Paul's when he received Timothy's positive report. But it is exciting to know that things are going well with those you love.

Zest for living (3:8). "For now we *really live,*" Paul responded, "since you are standing firm in the Lord" (3:8).

This statement has strong emotional overtones. Paul, of course, was not saying that they were literally "staying alive" because of Timothy's report. Rather he was saying, "We are so excited about what is happening to you that we have courage to go on teaching and preaching the gospel with a new fervor and excitement."

Have you ever felt that kind of motivation? I certainly have. There have been times when I have been personally discouraged in the ministry. Things just haven't gone well. I've wondered if anything was really happening in people's lives. Or, I've been fearful I've offended someone whom I have not seen recently at church. And then I receive a report of some unique way in which the Word of God has been at work in a Christian's life because of my own personal ministry—or the ministry of someone else. Or I discover there has been no offense. I've just been paranoid in my own thinking.

As a result of this information, I've actually sensed a new

surge of energy to go on in God's work—to prepare another message, to help someone in trouble, to encourage someone else, to make a telephone call that I have hesitated to make or to answer letters that are long overdue for response. Or even to confront someone who is living in sin and out of the will of God.

Paul was simply saying that the positive report regarding the Thessalonians gave him a new surge of energy, a new zest for living the Christian life, and a new motivation to carry on the ministry that God had called him to.

Joy (3:9). Joy, of course, is one of the most positive emotions a human being experiences. Paul experienced it. His anxiety was dissipated with a feeling of happiness. And so he wrote, "How can we thank God enough for you in return for all the *joy* we have in the presence of our God because of you?" (3:9).

Paul's perspective on joy was both present and future. Earlier he had written, "For what is our hope, our *joy,* or the crown in which we will glory in the presence of our Lord Jesus when he comes? Is it not you? Indeed you are our glory and joy" (2:19-20). Here Paul was referring to that day when they would together stand in the presence of Jesus Christ and rejoice together. The greatest joy for Paul would be to see these believers in heaven.

But Paul's joy was also a part of his earthly experience. And in this instance it was directly related to the way in which these believers had stood firm in their faith, in spite of persecution.

Paul's Reasons

Again, to understand more fully what Paul was actually feeling, we need to look more specifically at the reasons for his positive emotions.

1. Timothy had brought good news about the Thessalonian Christians' faith and love (3:6).

This report is why Paul began this letter by thanking God for their "work produced by faith" and the "labor prompted by love" (1:3). Timothy had just reported on the state of the Thessalonian church—and Paul was elated.

2. Timothy had reported that the Thessalonian Christians had "pleasant memories" and longed *"to see"* them again (3:6).

From a human point of view, this report probably lifted Paul's spirits more than anything. Paul and his fellow missionaries had demonstrated their love for these people in unusual ways. They had "worked night and day in order not to be a burden to anyone" (2:9). Like a nursing mother they had tenderly cared for them (2:7). Like a loving father they had nurtured them one by one (2:11-12). They had literally risked their lives so that they might share the gospel with these people (2:2).

To receive a report that these Christians had forgotten what Paul and his fellow missionaries had done or, worse yet, to hear that they had unpleasant memories would have devastated these men emotionally. So we can understand Paul's positive response. These people remembered and longed to see them again just as Paul, Silas and Timothy longed to see them.

Unfortunately, some people whom Paul had led to Christ did not respond positively to his ministry after he left them. The Corinthians are a primary example. In their carnality they rejected Paul. They rejected his apostolic authority and questioned his motives. In their immaturity they became followers of men rather than followers of Jesus Christ. This, of course, was a very painful experience for Paul and made it very difficult for him to confront them in the Corinthian letters (see 1 Cor. 1:10-17; 2 Cor. 1:12-21). But because Paul's love was unconditional, he confronted them nevertheless.

By way of application, people generally have very short memories regarding the good things others do for them. Selfishness and pride often blur our memories and cause us to purposely "forget" that we owe a great deal to others for our success. We gladly receive help when we are in a desperate situation, but then we conveniently forget to say thank you and to express our appreciation in other ways. What is even more tragic is when people who receive help refuse to help others who are in the same need they were at one time.

For a Christian, this kind of behavior is tragic and inexcusable. It is the absolute opposite of Christlike behavior. We of all people are to "live a life of love, just as Christ loved us and gave himself up for us" (Eph. 5:2).

Let us never forget where we've come from and also who helped us get there—our parents, a friend, a business associate, a teacher, a pastor, etc. And let us not forget to say thanks and to look for opportunities to share our appreciation in tangible ways.

I've often shared my sense of indebtedness to a professor at Moody Bible Institute named Harold Garner, who took me under his wing when I was both theologically and emotionally confused. My self-image was at a low ebb. But he believed in me when I didn't believe in myself. My ability to handle the English language was so poor I flunked an entrance test in composition. I couldn't even write a paragraph stating why I had come to Moody Bible Institute. It is hard for me to believe this now, but in those days I actually used phrases like "we done it" and "we was"—not really knowing that they were grammatically incorrect.

But Harold Garner saw potential in me—something I found very difficult to accept. He set a goal in front of me that I found difficult to take seriously. "Gene," he said on several occasions, "when you graduate from Moody Bible Institute, I want you to go to college and get an advanced degree. I want you to come back here some day and join this faculty to be my associate."

I found it difficult to set that goal, not because I didn't want to, but because I didn't think I could ever do it. But he kept encouraging me to go on for further education. Believe it or not, I did go back to Moody and join the faculty—because of *his* recommendation. In fact, I was the youngest man ever to join that faculty—as far as I know. I was only 23 years old—teaching college-level students. I still feel nervous when I think about it.

Humanly speaking, I owe most everything that I've been able to accomplish in the ministry to that one man. And I have tried never to forget it. He is with the Lord now. But over the years I wrote many notes and made many phone calls, just to say thanks. Every time I wrote a book I tried to remember to send a copy to him with a note, letting him know that if it were not for his encouragement I would still be saying "I done it" and "we was." Truly, if it were not for this man, I would not even have finished my education at Moody Bible Institute.

The point of this illustration is to encourage you to say thank you and to show appreciation to those who have helped you become what you are.

Even more tragic is the fact that some Christians do not say thank you to Jesus Christ. They take for granted what He has done for us. He gave everything. He died on the cross. He suffered the agony of a cruel death and bore the burden of our sins. And yet, as Christians, we tend to forget. We do not reciprocate. We do not present our bodies back to Him in appreciation for what He has done for us. When Christians treat Christ this way, it is not surprising that they will treat their fellow Christians in the same way.

The Thessalonians had a special place in Paul's heart. They had responded to these missionaries' love and never forgot that love. Consequently, Paul wrote, "In all our distress and persecution we were *encouraged*" (1 Thess. 3:7).

3. Timothy reported that these Christians were "standing firm in the Lord" (3:8).

Regarding their spiritual growth, Timothy reported on three major areas—their "work produced by faith," their "labor prompted by love" and their "endurance inspired by hope" (1 Thess. 1:3). "Standing firm in the Lord" relates directly to their "endurance inspired by hope." No one—false teachers, persecution or Satan himself—had diverted them from their hope in Jesus Christ. From a divine perspective, this was the greatest news Timothy reported. Paul's concern that they may have become "unsettled by these trials" (3:3) had been one of the major causes for Paul's anxiety.

Paul's Actions

When Paul experienced negative emotions, he took action. He sought solutions for the concerns that were creating so much anxiety. And when he experienced positive emotions which resulted from his earlier actions in sending Timothy to check on the Thessalonians' spiritual welfare, he also responded with specific steps of action.

1. Paul thanked God for this good report (3:9).

"How can we *thank God* enough for you in return for all the joy we have in the presence of our God because of you?" was Paul's initial response. He didn't take credit for the positive report. He didn't brag about his efforts. He didn't tell everyone what a wonderful ministry they had among these people and why it was so successful. Rather, he thanked God! Paul knew that all glory must go to God for even those things that involve our personal efforts. Ultimately, God must be glorified in all we do.

2. Paul continued to pray that he might see them again and help them even more (3:10-11).

You might think that Paul would have been satisfied with Timothy's report and desire to go on to greener pastures. Not so! He still wanted to see the Thessalonian Christians and encourage them even more. What a tremendous example of a man with a shepherd's heart!

3. Paul prayed for the Thessalonians' continued spiritual growth in love and holiness (3:12-13).

Paul's prayer speaks for itself: "May the Lord make your *love* increase and overflow for each other and for everyone else, just as ours does for you. May he strengthen your hearts so that you will be *blameless and holy* in the presence of our God and Father when our Lord Jesus comes with all his holy ones" (1 Thess. 3:12-13).

PRACTICAL LESSONS FROM PAUL'S EXPERIENCES

There are many lessons we can learn from Paul's openness in sharing his feelings in this section of his letter. Let's look at a few.

1. Negative emotions are normal.

In and of themselves they are not wrong, nor are they avoidable. But some may ask a question at this point. Did not Paul himself tell us not to be anxious? "Do not be anxious about anything, but in everything, by prayer and petition, with thanksgiving, present your requests to God. And the peace of God, which transcends all understanding, will guard your hearts and minds in Christ Jesus" (Phil. 4:6-7).

There are certain circumstances that are beyond our control.

Our only recourse is prayer and committing that burden to Jesus Christ. For example, the Thessalonians could not avoid persecution. And Paul's exhortation and promise to the Philippians was very applicable to their lives. However, Paul's concern and anxiety regarding the Thessalonians was something he could do something about himself—in addition to praying. To commit this to the Lord without committing himself to do what he could for them would be to neglect his responsibility toward them. Furthermore, he needed to find out what was actually happening to them in order to put his mind at ease. And this leads us to a second lesson.

2. Negative emotions, particularly, motivate us to take action.

If it were not for feelings of anxiety, we often would neglect our responsibility as parents or as business persons. Some of the great accomplishments happen because of fear and anxiety. That fact can be demonstrated again and again throughout history. In that sense, God uses negative emotions—and Paul's experience illustrates it.

Furthermore, we often worry about something because we don't have enough information about it. This was true of Paul. The resolution to his problem was to send Timothy to find out what was actually happening.

Some people avoid finding out what is happening for fear that what they fear is a reality, so they just go on worrying. Often the fear is unjustified. And even if it is based on reality, finding out what has caused the problem most often enables us to solve it and thereby overcome our fear and anxiety.

3. Not all roadblocks are God's way of saying no.

Some Christians are tempted to interpret all barriers to achieving difficult goals as God's barriers. "Obviously," they conclude, "if God wanted us to accomplish this goal, He would open the door and make it happen."

If this were true, why did Paul say, "For we wanted to come to you—certainly I, Paul, did again and again—but Satan stopped us" (1 Thess. 2:18)?

In this case it's clear that Satan was setting up the barrier. And Paul knew it and set up an alternate plan to achieve his goal. He did not give up.

In conjunction with this particular lesson, my mind goes back to something I learned several years ago when I was writing the official history of Moody Bible Institute in Chicago. In the course of my research I learned about a young man, a graduate of Yale University, who was at Moody in the 1920s. His name was Henry Coleman Crowell. Eventually he became assistant to the president, which gave him an opportunity to be very influential in the growth and development of this institution.

Henry Crowell had trained in the area of electronics while studying at Yale. So he was very much aware of the experimentation going on in the area of communicating messages via ether waves. And when the first radio broadcasts began to be transmitted from Pittsburgh, Pennsylvania, back in the early '20s, he immediately saw the way this could be used to further the cause of Christ. Consequently, he proposed to James M. Gray, who was president at the time, that Moody Bible Institute consider setting up their own radio station.

Young Crowell immediately faced resistance. In fact, President Gray initially feared that this new phenomenon might have something to do with the realm of Satan himself. After all, Paul talked about "the powers of this dark world" and "the spiritual forces of evil in the heavenly realms" (Eph. 6:12).

Henry Coleman Crowell was not a theologian, but he knew enough theology, plus he knew enough about science to know that this was not a satanic medium in itself. Certainly Satan could use the medium of radio—as he has—but the ability to transmit a message in this way was simply learning how to use God's laws for a good purpose.

Crowell did not give up. He continued his research, continued his communication with the president, and eventually convinced Dr. Gray to give permission to set up a radio station in Chicago.

But the problems were just beginning. This was a whole new set of circumstances in the world of communication. The Radio Commission in Washington, D.C. had not set up codes to control this kind of new development. Radio stations went on the air everywhere, some overlapping each other's frequencies. When Moody Bible Institute first went on the air in 1926, their radio signal overlapped the signal of one of the major radio stations in Chicago. In fact, both stations went on the air the same day. Intense pressure was brought to bear upon Moody Bible Institute to stop broadcasting.

As I researched this bit of history, I discovered some incredible things. For example, Henry Coleman Crowell made no less than 10 trips to Washington, D.C., during the first two years of broadcasting. Rather than simply going off the air, he went before the Radio Commission, offered alternate solutions and even gave them guidance in solving the problems that were emerging all over the United States. With each trip to Washington, he was given permission to continue broadcasting for a while longer.

Eventually the problem was solved and today Moody Bible Institute has its own sunlight to sunset AM frequency in Chicago. Had they given up initially, interpreting this gigantic hurdle as God's way of saying they shouldn't go on the air, they would have lost one of the greatest opportunities this institution has ever had. Radio Station WMBI now is a model for others in Christian radio broadcasting, and currently has radio stations broadcasting its programs from many different points in the United States. Recently WMBI began to use satellite communications, multiplying their radio outreach many times.

The lesson that came to me from this experience is to remember that not all barriers are created by God. Some of them may just be natural barriers that have to be overcome. And Paul's experience demonstrates that Satan himself can become active in attempting to keep us from doing what God wants us to do. In these cases, Paul persevered, and so should we.

4. Let us be sure to follow through with proper action when we achieve our goals and experience positive emotions.

How easy it is to stop pursuing the opportunities God gives us when things are going well. We tend to settle down and be happy with the status quo. Paul and his co-workers illustrate dramatically that the same good news which brings encouragement, joy and happiness should also increase our zest for living and our desire to achieve more and more for God. It should also intensify our prayer life. Let us thank God continually for the good things He accomplishes for us and through us. And let us continue to pray for ourselves and others, that we all might continue in spiritual growth, reflecting God's love and holiness.

Notes
1. Though Paul used the editorial "we" in this section, some believe he was actually referring to his personal feelings throughout. This seems to be verified in 1 Thessalonians 2:18 and 3:5, where Paul used the singular pronoun "I." Since Paul had been using the plural pronouns to this point in this letter to refer to Timothy and Silas, as well as himself, it would be natural for him to continue using these pronouns, even though he was referring primarily to his own feelings at this juncture in the letter.
2. There is some ambiguity regarding the phrase translated "again and again." It can be literally translated "once and twice." However, many believe that Paul was referring to a number of occasions.

8

Living to Please God

1 THESSALONIANS 4:1-12

¹Finally, brothers, we instructed you how to live in order to please God, as in fact you are living. Now we ask you and urge you in the Lord Jesus to do this more and more. ²You know what instructions we gave you by the authority of the Lord Jesus.

³It is God's will that you should be holy; that you should avoid sexual immorality; ⁴that each of you should learn to control his own body in a way that is holy and honorable, ⁵not in passionate lust like the heathen, who do not know God; ⁶and that in this matter no one should wrong his brother or take advantage of him. The Lord will punish men for all such sins, as we have already told you and warned you. ⁷For God did not call us to be impure, but to live a holy life. ⁸Therefore, he who rejects this instruction does not reject man but God, who gives you his Holy Spirit.

⁹Now about brotherly love we do not need to write to you, for you yourselves have been taught by God to love each other. ¹⁰And in fact, you do love all the brothers throughout Macedonia. Yet we urge you, brothers, to do so more and more.

¹¹Make it your ambition to lead a quiet life, to mind your own business and to work with your hands, just as we told you, ¹²so that your daily life may win the respect of outsiders and so that you will not be dependent on anybody.

The very week I was studying this passage (1 Thess. 4:1-12) and writing this chapter, I watched a popular news broadcast, "Nightline." The subject was pornography. I was particularly interested in hearing what was said because of the subject Paul treats in 1 Thessalonians 4:3-8.

Four guests appeared on this program. One was a woman lawyer who proposed stricter laws governing pornography. Her concerns were based primarily on a concern for women's rights. A feminist, she was representing thousands of her kind who believe women are being used, abused and placed in subservient positions by the producers of pornographic books and films.

Another guest was a well-known author who has researched the sexual behavior of Americans, using both techniques of observation and personal participation. This published report is so graphic it would be classified by many as pornography in and of itself.

A third guest was a minister who opposed the proposed law by the feminist attorney because it would immediately classify certain popular R-rated films as illegal because of explicit sexual scenes—an action he believes would be a violation of human rights.

The fourth guest was an older woman who claimed that she grew up in a home where she was sexually abused because of pornography. She further related that her daughter experienced the same abuse because young men in the neighborhood were acting out what they had been reading and seeing in pornographic materials.

Thirty minutes later—at the end of the program—they had reached no conclusions. If anything, they had confused the issue even more. Incidentally, the person who received the least amount of time to express her views was the abused woman who had been a victim of pornography.

As I listened and watched and later reflected on what I had heard and seen, it became increasingly clear that moral values were not an issue in the discussion. This lack was of particular interest to me since one participant was a minister. In the entire discussion, a higher authority than man himself was not even considered. The purely pragmatic dialogue was rooted in secular humanism. Biblical presuppositions and standards—historically the bedrock of American life and laws—were not even alluded to.

Ronald Allen in his book *The Majesty of Man* states clearly the reason for this dilemma in our society today, particularly as it relates to an issue such as pornography. He writes:

> When man is the measure of all things,
>   there is no need for God;
> With the loss of faith, Being is beggard;
>   there is really no meaning for man—
> Hence, grab, get, and glut!
> Eat, drink and be merry!
>   for you only go around once.[1]

When Paul and his two missionary companions entered the city of Thessalonica, they faced a philosophy of life that was very similar to our own today. Though they found a Jewish synagogue, the values of the Old Testament had made little impact upon the Gentiles who lived in this pagan city. Furthermore, the Jews themselves had been so tainted and influenced by the Greek and Roman culture that they had no clear-cut witness in this sinful society.

However, through the power of the gospel and the regenerating work of the Holy Spirit, many of these people—both Jews and Gentiles—had been converted to Jesus Christ and a new way of life. In fact, Paul, Silas and Timothy began immediately to teach these people how to live for Christ. "Finally, brothers, we instructed you *how to live in order to please God,* as in fact you are living" (1 Thess. 4:1).

However, Paul was never satisfied with the level of maturity either in his own life or in the lives of other believers. Therefore, he went on to say, "Now we ask you and urge you in the Lord Jesus to do this *more and more."* Furthermore, he reminded them that the instructions they had given these people regarding living a Christian life-style were not based on their own viewpoint and convictions. Rather he said, "You know what instructions we gave you *by the authority of the Lord Jesus"* (4:2).

What Paul stated in the next few verses of this letter does

not represent a human point of view. It is not based on Paul's authority—even as an apostle. It represents God's point of view. Paul's authority in these matters was Jesus Christ Himself. Any arguments or resistance the Thessalonian Christians had with Paul's teachings must be recognized as a disagreement with Almighty God who has said on numerous occasions, "Be holy as I am holy." And so it is with any Christian in the twentieth-century world.

Let's look at how to live in order to please God—*then* and *now!*

LIVING A HOLY LIFE

Paul makes immediately clear in this paragraph (1 Thess. 4:3-8) that holiness is identified, indeed is synonymous, with sexual purity. He writes, "It is God's will that you should be *holy;* that you should avoid sexual immorality; that each of you should learn to control his own body in a way that is holy and honorable" (4:3-4).

Life-styles: Pagan vs. Christian

Extra-marital sexual relations were accepted as the norm in the pagan culture of New Testament times. Ceremonial prostitution was part of the religious system. Fornication and adultery were common practices.

Men, particularly, took sexual liberties with women other than their wives. Though polygamy—having more than one wife—was outlawed in the Roman Empire, men commonly had prostitutes they would visit regularly. Often a slave owner would have sexual relations with a slave girl on a regular basis, because she was accessible to him in the same home he shared with his legal spouse.

Wives, of course, knew all about their husbands' sexual behavior. However, because they could do little if anything about them, they accepted these practices as part of life. They had no other options open to them before the arrival of the Christian gospel.

The message of Christianity brought with it a whole new point of view to those caught up in this licentious life-style. The message was one of sexual purity—a reiteration, of course, of the laws God had given to Israel years before. "You shall not commit adultery," God had thundered from Mount Sinai. "You shall not covet your neighbor's wife" (Exod. 20:14,17).

And in reiterating God's laws, Paul contrasted Christ's message of holiness with that of the pagan world. A Christian must not give in to "passionate lust like the heathen, who do not know God" (1 Thess. 4:5).

Sexual Sin Is Not Sin Against God Alone

In a stricter sense, sexual sin is certainly a sin against our brothers and sisters in Christ. But here Paul indicates that sexual sin is sin against any person who participates in sinful activities. People who engage in illicit sexual relations are sinning against each other. "In this matter," Paul wrote, "no one should wrong his brother or take advantage of him" (4:6). Here the term "brother" is generic, referring to "brother man" or "sister woman." The reference is to mankind.

In their own way, many American feminists recognize this "sinning against" factor in their reaction to pornography. Though many of these women may reject God's standard of morality, they nevertheless are verifying the consequences of violating God's standards: the violation of the other person. They see the results, the dehumanizing that takes place, particularly of women. But because they are reacting to effect rather than to cause, many do not acknowledge the reasons why they feel the way they do about pornography. The majority, no doubt, do not understand the "why" at all.

God Will Ultimately Judge Sexual Sin

Paul next reminded the Thessalonians that "the Lord will punish men for all such sins" (1 Thess. 4:6). While with them in Thessalonica Paul had already emphasized this point and warned these new Christians against continuing in their old practices.

It is clear from many Scriptures that God will ultimately judge sexual sins. But it is also true that God will eventually discipline His own children if they continue to violate His laws in this matter (see Heb. 12:7-11). Paul made it clear that his warning was directed to both non-Christians and Christians when he wrote, "For God did not call us to be impure, but to live a holy life. Therefore, he who rejects this instruction does not reject man but God, who gives you his Holy Spirit" (1 Thess. 4:7-8). Though God is very long-suffering and forgiving in these matters, eventually we reap what we sow (Gal. 6:7).

Note that Paul was not condemning sex per se. Over the years some well-meaning Christians have found it very difficult to differentiate between legitimate sex and illegitimate sex. Some have even classified the original sin as a sexual sin! This view is very unfortunate for the Bible presents sex as God-created and a means not only for procreation, but as a marvelous expression of love.

God also designed sex to be physically enjoyable and emotionally satisfying. He goes further and even classified the sexual act between a husband and wife as a symbolic expression of the oneness that exists between Jesus Christ and the Church (Eph. 5:22-33). So Christians, of all people, should be free to enjoy sex as God has designed it.

Paul then was teaching against *improper* sexual expression—sexual relations outside the bonds of marriage. Within God's scheme of things we read that "marriage should be honored by all, and the marriage bed kept pure, for God will judge the adulterer and all the sexually immoral" (Heb. 13:4).

LIVING A LIFE OF LOVE

Again Paul commended the Thessalonians for their response to his teaching. In fact, they had continued to grow in brotherly love even after Paul, Silas and Timothy had left them. Thus Paul wrote, "Now about *brotherly love* we do not need to write to you, for you yourselves have been taught by God to *love* each other. And in fact, you do *love* all the brothers throughout Macedonia" (1 Thess. 4:9-10).

But again, Paul was not satisfied. He made it clear that none of us as Christians has or ever will love others as Christ has loved us. Therefore, Christ's love should be a constant goal; so Paul again challenged them with these words, "Yet we urge you, brothers, to do so *more and more*" (4:10).

The hallmark of true Christian maturity among Christians is not only sexual purity, but brotherly love. These two concepts, of course, are not unrelated. True love for a brother and sister in Christ—outside of our marriage partner—should not be sexual. Though it involves a deep sense of friendship, affectionate feelings and unselfish caring, it must never involve sexual stimulation.

At this point it is important to understand God's total perspective on love. There are two Greek words used in the New Testament for love. Paul used both in these two verses.

Agapao Love

The word used most frequently in the New Testament is *agapao* or *agape* love. Paul used this word twice when he wrote, "For you yourselves have been taught by God to *love* each other. And in fact, you do *love* all the brothers throughout Macedonia" (4:9-10).

In most instances New Testament writer used *agapao* to portray *loving acts*—that is, behaving in certain ways because it is the *right thing* to do. This is the kind of love that is defined in 1 Corinthians 13 as being "patient" and "kind." This kind of love "does not envy, it does not boast" and "it is not proud." Furthermore, "it is not rude, it is not self-seeking, it is not easily angered, it keeps no record of wrongs." It "does not delight in evil but rejoices with the truth. It always protects, always trusts, always hopes, always perseveres" (1 Cor. 13:4-7).

Phileo Love

Another word used in the Greek New Testament for love is *phileo*. Though it is used interchangeably at times with *agapao*, it seemingly also has a distinctive meaning. It is associated with true friendship. Perhaps one of the best definitions of this kind of love is "a deep emotional feeling of trust generated from one person to another person."²

As Paul wrote to the Thessalonians he made reference to this kind of love. The Greek word translated "brotherly love" which Paul used in verse 9 is the word *philadelphia*. In context it is clear that Paul was referring to the loving, sensitive and caring relationship that should exist among brothers and sisters in Jesus Christ. The Thessalonian Christians had already excelled in this kind of love.

Erao Love

There was another word for "love" that was used by Greek-speaking people in the first century. It was the word *erao*. Usually it referred to sexual relationships. Interestingly, this word was never used by New Testament authors, although this is the kind of relationship Paul was dealing with in 1 Thess. 4:3-8 when he discussed sexual immorality.

As we have already pointed out, this does not mean that sexual love was considered wrong or improper or that it is never referred to in the New Testament. However, biblical writers no doubt avoided this word because it was so frequently used in their culture to describe illicit sexual activity. Though it is not a totally accurate comparison, there are certain words for sexual expressions in our present-day culture that we avoid in most proper public discussions of sexual love. Though these words are frequently used by people to describe and talk about illicit sex in literature, movies and jokes, they are considered unacceptable, particularly by those who treat sex as sacred.

A Three-Dimensional Perspective

The Scriptures, then, present the concept of love as three dimensional. In its broadest meaning it involves attitudes and actions that are right and proper no matter how we feel (see fig. 1). *Agapao* love rises above feelings that may be more negative than positive. This is the kind of love that Jesus Christ demonstrated when He, with an act of His will, chose the cross in spite of the agony He faced (see Luke 22:42). This was the ultimate in *agapao* love.

Phileo love involves positive feelings and should always be a part of and guided by *agapao* love (again see fig. 1). In fact, it is *agapao* love that keeps feelings of affection from becoming selfish and demanding. Many friendships have been destroyed by people who try to keep a relationship purely to themselves.

Furthermore, it is *agapao* love that keeps the feelings of *phileo* love toward a family member or a brother and sister in Christ from becoming illicit, resulting in incest, homosexuality, fornication and adultery.

The Thessalonians were an example in the area of *phileo* love. They were responding to each other's needs affectionately and with positive emotions, but within the guidelines of *agapao* love.

Again, it should be underscored that erotic feelings and actions are also part of the circle of biblical love. *Erao* love has been designed by God to be used and enjoyed fully, but it is always to be expressed within the boundaries of *agapao* and *phileo* love—in short, a marital relationship between a man and a woman (again see fig. 1). It is this larger context that keeps a relationship morally on track. And it is love expressed only in this larger context that will keep these feelings from being used in purely selfish ways, even in a marital relationship. Furthermore, it is this larger context that helps Christian couples keep their emotional equilibrium during the many times when life together is difficult and demanding.[3]

LIVING A RESPECTABLE LIFE

In this section of his letter (1 Thess. 4:11-12) Paul exhorted the Thessalonians in another area regarding how to live in order to please God. Paul wrote, "Make it your ambition to lead a quiet life, to mind your own business and to work with your hands" (4:11).

The Thessalonians evidently had a problem which resulted

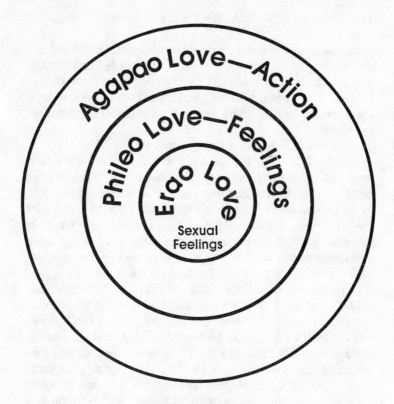

THE CIRCLE OF
BIBLICAL LOVE

Doing what is *right* and *best* for someone, even if it involves
negative feelings.

Responding to someone's needs affectionately and with
positive emotions, but always within the guidelines of
agape love.

Becoming both emotionally and physically involved with
another person sexually, but always within the guidelines of
agape and *phileo* love.

Figure 1

from a false view of the second coming of Christ. Some used this doctrine to justify their not working, so they relied on others to meet their physical needs. Evidently, they were rationalizing, telling themselves that since Christ was coming back to take them home to heaven, there was no need to get involved in making a living.

This problem did not go away easily for the Thessalonians. In fact, Paul picked up the same theme in his second letter. "We hear that some among you are idle," he wrote. "They are not busy; they are busybodies. Such people we command and urge in the Lord Jesus Christ to settle down and earn the bread they eat" (2 Thess. 3:11-12). In fact, Paul became very direct in reminding them of something he and the others had taught these people when they were with them. "We gave you this rule," he said. "If a man will not work, he shall not eat" (3:10).

There is evidence from Paul's statement in 1 Thessalonians 4:11-12 that many of these Christians in Thessalonica were of the artisan class. They were not wealthy people. Paul's statement indicates that they came from the lower strata of society, since manual labor among the Greeks was looked down on as beneath them, and the Jews viewed manual labor as a responsibility of slaves. Some of the Thessalonian Christians evidently took their position in Christ to an impractical extreme and decided to fold their hands rather than to continue working with their hands.

There is a positive note here, however. Remember, Paul commended the Macedonian churches for their work of faith— the way in which they gave of what they had out of their poverty (2 Cor. 8:1-4). The majority evidently were very diligent people. Though they had little, they shared much.

However, there were some who needed this exhortation to be diligent. And Paul made it clear as to why he was concerned that they be diligent in making a living. He did not want their lifestyle to be a stumbling block to those who did not know Christ (1 Thess. 4:12). Furthermore, he did not want them to take advantage of their brothers and sisters in Christ (4:12).

One final and related thought about Paul's exhortation is to be busy in carrying out our daily responsibilities. Idleness is frequently the devil's workshop—particularly in terms of morality. This is one reason Paul warned young widows in the New Testament church not to "get into the habit of being idle and going about from house to house" (1 Tim. 5:13).

This was also part of King David's problem when he committed adultery with Bathsheba. It happened at a time when "kings go off to war." But "David remained in Jerusalem" (2 Sam. 11:1). He was idle and not about the business of leading his people. And though he had access to multiple wives (a practice God permitted but did not approve as His perfect will for men and women), he evidently was seeking some *new* experience, a *new* sexual thrill, a *new* woman. He was attracted to Bathsheba's sensuality and though he is classified as a man after God's heart, he committed a horrible sin against God and the people of Israel. The consequences of his sin were devastating to David and his family.

We see somewhat of a parallel in our own workaholic society. A man's most sexually vulnerable moments come when he puts his mind in neutral—particularly after a period of stress and emotional exertion. It's during such times that we must be on guard against temptation.

Don't misunderstand! I'm not suggesting we don't need leisure time. I am suggesting that in view of societal expectations, and in view of the incredible number of possibilities for sexual stimulation in our society, we must be on guard against Satan.

PLEASING GOD IN THE TWENTIETH-CENTURY WORLD

Several years ago the slogan "You've come a long way baby" was used to promote the fact that women had finally gained the right to join men in using substances that are readily recognized as being harmful. But that slogan has far greater implications today. It reflects a changing culture—one that has in many respects moved from being God-centered at least in principle to being man-centered in almost all facets of life. Put another way, we are rapidly becoming a secular society. *We* are our own authority. And that is why the television discussion on pornography referred to earlier ended in greater confusion than when it began.

Ronald Allen succinctly captures what has been and is still happening in our society when he wrote:

> We are in a new world and not just because of the computer. For those of us who live in North America, that new world has come with stunning rapidity. As in the case of children at Disneyland we have hardly had time to catch our breath before we are on a new adventure. But unlike Disneyland, not all of the adventures are pleasant. Many of us find these new adventures difficult to accept. The new world has us reeling.
>
> Think of the changes in our new world and the mores expressed in the popular arts. Can it be that less than 25 years ago, Allen Drury's daring novel *Advise and Consent* turned on the dilemma of a public figure being exposed as a homosexual? Such a plot line would hardly cause a ripple today.[4]

As I was writing this chapter, an article appeared in the *Dallas Morning News* reviewing a stage play being performed at a publicly funded theatre. The play, entitled *Torch Song Trilogy,* featured open and blatant homosexuality—and certain scenes were so graphically described in the article that I feel it would be inappropriate to repeat them in this chapter.[5]

But what about illicit heterosexual behavior in our society? Again, Allen focuses the dramatic changes that have taken place: "Can anyone who has seen current situation comedy on television believe that such programs could have come within three decades of 'Ozzie and Harriet' or 'I Love Lucy'? It is a new world. It is an uncomfortable world for those who cherish fidelity and constancy in marriage (between a man and a woman!). In this new world the values of traditional biblical morality are the new endangered species."[6]

While teaching a summer course at an evangelical seminary

on the West Coast, I was informed by the president of the school that he had just seen a report on television regarding the use of video to reproduce pornographic films. Cameras took the television audience to a pornographic production center where 600 video machines were reproducing X-rated materials 24 hours a day. And this, of course, represents only one such operation.

WHAT IS A CHRISTIAN TO DO?

I personally applaud those who are attempting to control pornography in our society. And I certainly want to do what I can to clean up society in order to protect our children and youth from this incredible exploitation. But I am concerned at another level. I am concerned about my own walk with Jesus Christ. I'm concerned about my family and the people I minister to and influence. To live in such a way so as to please God, we have no choice but to be obedient to the Word of God.

We must commit ourselves to God's standard of morality and not allow ourselves to be conformed to the world's system. If we falter here we will ultimately pay a terrible price. We will "reap what we sow" (Gal. 6:7). Moral compromise is a downhill experience (read Rom. 1).

At this juncture Paul's words to the Philippians are extremely relevant in our twentieth-century culture. They were written to people who lived in a culture that was permeated with sexual immorality. "Finally, brothers, whatever is *true,* whatever is *noble,* whatever is *right,* whatever is *pure,* whatever is *lovely,* whatever is *admirable*—if anything is excellent or praiseworthy—think about such things" (Phil. 4:8).

We must encourage one another to live holy lives. No Christian can fight this battle alone. I know I can't. And neither can you. We need mutual encouragement to live holy lives.

Notes

1. From the book *The Majesty of Man* by Ronald B. Allen, copyright 1984 by Multnomah Press, Portland, Oregon 97266. Used by permission.
2. Reprinted with permission from "Living Together" by Mort Katz, Ms., Farnsworth Publishing Co., Rockville Centre, NY, © 1982.
3. For a more in-depth treatment of this subject see Gene A. Getz, *The Measure of a Marriage* (Ventura, CA: Regal Books, 1980), ch. 9.
4. Ronald Allen, *The Majesty of Man*, p. 18. Used by permission.
5. To be fair the article was a reaction against the production, deploring the use of a publicly funded theatre to stage the play.
6. Allen, *The Majesty of Man*, p. 18. Used by permission.

9

Paul's Words of Encouragement

1 THESSALONIANS 4:13-18

¹³Brothers, we do not want you to be ignorant about those who fall asleep, or to grieve like the rest of men, who have no hope. ¹⁴We believe that Jesus died and rose again and so we believe that God will bring with Jesus those who have fallen asleep in him. ¹⁵According to the Lord's own word, we tell you that we who are still alive, who are left till the coming of the Lord, will certainly not precede those who have fallen asleep. ¹⁶For the Lord himself will come down from heaven, with a loud command, with the voice of the archangel and with the trumpet call of God, and the dead in Christ will rise first. ¹⁷After that, we who are still alive and are left will be caught up with them in the clouds to meet the Lord in the air. And so we will be with the Lord forever. ¹⁸Therefore encourage each other with these words.

The passage of Scripture we want to discuss in this chapter (1 Thess. 4:13-18) becomes very meaningful to me every time I conduct a funeral for a Christian. Furthermore, I try to make it as meaningful and comforting as I can for the family, always using the occasion as an opportunity to share with the family and all those who attend the funeral why death for a Christian can and should be a celebration rather than a time of hopelessness.

Don't misunderstand! Losing a loved one is always painful. It's a time of deep sorrow and sadness—particularly if the death is sudden or premature from a human point of view. And sometimes it raises questions in our minds we cannot really answer completely.

Let me share a very deep personal experience that helps illustrate what I mean and I trust will also set the stage for a careful look at Paul's teaching in this next section of his letter.

When I was a student at Moody Bible Institute I met a young woman I cared for very deeply. Though I had my share of dating experiences while I was growing up, never before had I been so attracted to a young woman. First of all, and most important to me, she loved Jesus Christ. I really admired her for months before I got up enough nerve to ask her out. And once we began dating, I began to ask myself that serious question: Is this the girl I'm going to marry?

But it never happened! She suddenly became ill. She developed a fever that just wouldn't go away. The school doctors were puzzled and finally decided she should leave school and go home to Denver where her parents and her family physician could give special attention to her illness.

I remember taking her to the train in downtown Chicago, helping her with her luggage and saying good-bye. Little did I realize that a couple of months later—the next time I would be able to see her—I would hardly recognize her lovely face. Her mother, knowing I was planning to come to Denver to visit her, had written to me, trying to prepare me.

But when I walked into the room where she was lying in bed, I wasn't really prepared. Her face was covered with scabs that marred her once beautiful complexion. Much of her lovely, long, flowing hair was gone. I still remember her embarrassed and nervous expression when I first entered the room; she was wondering how I would react to these dramatic changes in her physical appearance.

I *was* shocked! The Lord gave me unusual grace to keep those feelings under control and somewhat hidden. But in that weakened and scarred body I continued to see a beautiful person—one whom I cared for dearly.

I spent nearly a week with her, trying to lift her spirits. As I left to return to school in Chicago, I knew her condition was serious, but I didn't know the extent of it. Over the next couple of months I continued to write her regularly. Then, on the very day I was to graduate from Moody, I received a letter from her mother. I remember sitting in my room, reflecting on what I had read—again not prepared for the message in that letter.

Mildred's family had taken her to the famed Mayo Clinic where she had been diagnosed as having a very rare but terminal disease that attacks the nervous system of young women—particularly in their teens or early 20s. They gave her one year to live—five at the most. "Lord," I thought, as I sat weeping uncontrollably, *"why* on graduation day?"

But God in His mercy also turned that period in her life into a blessing. Just a couple of months after her mother wrote to me, Mildred was with the Lord Jesus Christ in heaven.

As a young man just 19, I faced the reality of death for the first time. But I also experienced in my life the reality of some biblical truth I had only read about before. The girl I loved had died. My human dreams were unfulfilled. The first person I had really cared about deeply was gone.

It was then my Christian faith was put to the test in many ways. Questions flooded my mind. Because of my knowledge of what God says about the death of His children, I knew where this young woman was. She was with Jesus Christ. I never doubted that great truth for a moment.

But there were other questions—questions that were not as easy to answer. Why had God let this happen? I was even tempted to wonder if God was punishing me for something in my own life—a thought I know now came from only one source—Satan himself.

There were other questions. Would God ever replace this person in my life? Would I ever be able emotionally to take a chance again? Over and over I asked myself, "What if this happened again?"

I know now that these are normal questions. And, of course, God did bring healing and another wonderful person into my life, a person whom I love more than anyone on earth. I didn't have the privilege of meeting her until I came back to Moody Bible Institute as a professor. Elaine was a student, and we were married two days after she graduated.

Death brings questions. Some are very difficult to answer. Some we *cannot* answer. But there are those we can answer, and with certainty! And so it was with the Thessalonian Christians. When Timothy returned from visiting this church, he related their questions about death to Paul. And in this passage, 1 Thessalonians 4:13-18, Paul answers one of these questions: *What happens to a Christian who dies before Christ comes again?*

CHRISTIANS WHO DIE HAVE HOPE

Paul answered this question directly and specifically. "Brothers," he wrote, "we do not want you to be ignorant about those who fall asleep, or to grieve like the rest of men, who have no hope" (1 Thess. 4:13). Here, "fall asleep" is used figuratively to refer to a person who had died. Jesus used this terminology in describing Lazarus's death (John 11:11-14).

It appears that, since Paul and his missionary companions had left Thessalonica, some of the Thessalonian believers had died. Even though Paul had instructed them regarding the second coming of Christ, there were still some things they didn't understand. They understood that Christ was coming again. In fact, people everywhere were telling Paul, Silas and Timothy how these people had "turned to God from idols to serve the living and true God, and to wait *for his Son from heaven*" (1 Thess. 1:9-10). But they did *not* understand that Christ might not come immediately and that, in the meantime, some of their loved ones would die. *What would happen to them?*

The answer to this question seems obvious to us. But we

must remember that many of these people were converted from idolatry. The idea of a personal Saviour who would return to take them home to heaven was a radical idea. That marvelous truth helps explain why some of them stopped working and decided to wait for Jesus Christ to deliver them from their difficult situation on earth (4:11-12).

Paul's answer to the question was that all Christians have hope—whether we live or die! Therefore, he continued, "We believe that Jesus died and rose again and so we believe that God will bring with Jesus those who have fallen asleep in him" (4:14).

At this point Paul began to explain a wonderful truth. Those who die go immediately to be with Jesus Christ. This is why Paul wrote to the Corinthians that "to be away from the body" is to be "at home with the Lord" (2 Cor. 5:8).

True, the body remains on earth and soon decays and returns to dust. But the spirit goes to be with the Lord. This is why Stephen, who was dying at the hands of cruel men, cried out, "Lord Jesus, receive my spirit" (Acts 7:59). This is also why Jesus could turn to the thief on the cross, who in those final minutes believed on the Lord Jesus Christ, and say, "I tell you the truth, *today* you will be with me in paradise" (Luke 23:43). Obviously, that converted criminal's body went into a tomb, but he—the real person—went to heaven to be with Christ.

Paul made another point clear in this verse. When Jesus comes again, those who have already died will come with Jesus when He returns (1 Thess. 4:14). At that moment the old body will be resurrected a new body. Writing to the Corinthians, Paul said that the dead will be "raised imperishable" (1 Cor. 15:42).

And let us not be concerned about such questions as to how this can happen when a body has been cremated and scattered in the wind. If God can save us and give us a body that will never perish when He comes again, He can certainly handle the problem of burial and what happens to our dust.

This paragraph and others we've already studied, speak directly to the false doctrine which is often called "soul sleep." There are those who teach that, when a Christian dies, the soul is in an unconscious state waiting for Christ to return.

Not so! Listen to Paul's testimony as he faced the prospect of death in a Roman prison. There is no question as to what he believed and taught regarding the immediate destiny of a Christian who dies: "For to me, to live is Christ and to die is gain. If I am to go on living in the body, this will mean fruitful labor for me. Yet what shall I choose? I do not know! I am torn between the two: I desire *to depart and be with Christ,* which is better by far; but it is more necessary for you that I *remain in the body* (Phil. 1:21-24).

Listen to D.L. Moody's testimony regarding this great truth. Realizing that he soon would be gone from this world, Moody said to a friend, "Someday you will read in the papers that D.L. Moody of Northfield is dead. Don't you believe a word of it.

"At that moment I shall be more alive than I am now. I shall have gone higher, that is all—out of this old clay tenement into a house that is immortal, a body that sin cannot touch, that sin cannot taint, a body fashioned into His glorious body. I was born in the flesh in 1836; I was born of the Spirit in 1856. That which is born of the flesh may die; that which is born of the Spirit will live forever."[1]

CHRISTIANS WHO LIVE HAVE HOPE

Paul emphasized in this next passage that *"we who are still alive,* who are left until the coming of the Lord, will certainly not precede those who have fallen asleep" (1 Thess. 4:15). Though we have hope and will be taken to heaven when Christ returns, our hope will not be greater than those who have died prior to this great event.

Paul explains (4:16) why this is true and how it will actually happen. "For the Lord Himself will come down from heaven,
- with a loud command,
- with the voice of the archangel and
- with the trumpet call of God."

At this moment, *"the dead in Christ will rise first. After that,"* Paul continued, "we who are still alive and left will be caught up with them in the clouds to meet the Lord in the air. And so we will be with the Lord forever" (4:16-17).

In answering this question, "What happens to a Christian who dies before Christ comes again?" Paul made it perfectly clear that both those who *die* in Christ and those who are *alive* in Christ will be of equal status when He comes again. We will go to meet the Lord "together." That means that if Christ came this very moment, my little sister Joanne, who died nearly 50 years ago of acute appendicitis when she was just three years old, will be right there with me—maybe by my side! We'll both have new bodies—glorified bodies—that will never again deteriorate.

As I reflect on this wonderful prospect, I can't help wondering what Joanne's body will look like. The last time I saw her, she was a pretty little three-year-old with beautiful blond hair that I loved to brush and comb as we sat in the backyard of our old farm home. The last time she saw me I was four, and had, believe it or not, thick, curly hair—most of which is now long gone! Yes, I really wonder what we'll look like in that day!

A CHRISTIAN'S ENCOURAGING HOPE

Paul concludes this section of his letter with an exhortation—"Therefore encourage each other with these words" (4:18).

Today as believers we know far more about God's great scheme of things because of His completed revelation in the Bible. There are still unanswered questions, because God doesn't want us to know everything about the future. In fact, Jesus Himself said, "No one knows about that day or hour, not even the angels in heaven, nor the Son, but only the Father" (Matt. 24:36). Therefore, it is inappropriate to set dates as some Christians have tried to do throughout the years. But one thing we know—Jesus *could* come at any moment. Paul thought Christ would come in his lifetime. What about our lifetime— nearly 2,000 years later?

But the main point Paul was making about the Second Coming is that for Christians, it will be a glorious day whether we are alive or have died when it happens. Even more important, Paul was writing to encourage Christians whose loved ones had died in Christ. We should be encouraged for at least two reasons.

First, our loved ones who have died in Christ are with Jesus. Though we may miss them greatly, they are far better off than we are.

Second, we'll see them again. We'll be reunited, not only in heaven, but on the way up! Those Christians who were alive and well in Thessalonica had nothing to be concerned about. Their loved ones who had died were safe in the arms of Jesus. Someday they would be together again, rejoicing in the presence of God. And so it will be someday for all of us as believers!

One of the greatest privileges I've ever had was to preach my dad's funeral sermon. I had not seen him for several months when we received word of his death. He died at age 78, doing what he loved most—driving the tractor on our family farm in Indiana. He suffered a heart attack and the tractor swerved off and hit a pine tree. The engine died and my mother found him still sitting on the tractor seat with his hands quietly resting on his lap. In the summer of 1984, my son Kenton and I visited the family farm and stood at the very spot where he died. My mother had placed a little marker under that tree indicating the spot where it happened. It was a neat experience for both of us.

When my own family received word of Dad's death, we immediately flew to Indiana for the funeral. I remember walking into the funeral home where his body was available for viewing. When I first saw him, my heart was instantly filled with grief. There lay my father. Tears welled up in my eyes and it was difficult for me to accept the fact that he was no longer alive. At that moment, I wished that I had been able to have just one more conversation with him.

But as I passed through those initial minutes of grief, I remembered what we had talked about so often when we were together—the hope we both had in Jesus Christ. He particularly enjoyed talking about the second coming of Christ. My grief began to subside as I realized that my father was not really residing in the body I was viewing. In a sense, Christ had already come for him. More accurately, of course, he had gone to be with Christ which Paul said was far better than to remain on earth (Phil. 1:23).

As I reached out to touch him, I knew I was only touching

the "home" he had lived in for 78 years. My dad's spirit was in heaven with Jesus—and far better off at that moment than I was. In the midst of my own tears I was sure that he was in that place where there were no tears—only eternal joy and happiness.

Someday God will bring Dad "with Jesus" to take all those who are yet alive to be with the Lord forever. Together the "dead in Christ" and those "who are still alive" will be "caught up . . . in the clouds to meet the Lord in the air." My dad's soul will be reunited with his body—a new body. Once again we will be able to converse together, but this time in the presence of the Lord.

Did that truth make any difference at that moment in my life? It made all the difference in the world—for me and my whole family! That knowledge and understanding enabled me to calmly stand before a large audience the next day and preach my dad's funeral message. There I announced with all certainty that my dad had gone home to be with the Lord Jesus Christ. Though I was grieving, I was not grieving as those who had no hope! Nor was my family.

Paul told the Thessalonian Christians to "encourage each other with these words." That's what I was doing that day for the Christians in my hometown. Paul was not denying that there would be sorrow over the death of loved ones. Rather, he was telling them that their grief was different. Their separation was only temporary. They would be reunited again when Jesus Christ comes to take *all* His children home to heaven—those who have died and those who are still alive.

As a pastor I have stood in similar situations, preaching funeral sermons for Christians who have lost loved ones. And again and again, I have shared this basic message of encouragement. One of my most rewarding experiences is to be able to see joy expressed through tears. How tragic for those ministers who can only eulogize but have nothing to say about eternity. And this leads to some very important questions.

ETERNAL QUESTIONS

What about your personal relationship with Jesus Christ? Do you know Him? Have you received Him? Do you have this hope? Do your children have this hope?

You *can* have this hope by receiving Jesus Christ as your personal Saviour, just as the Thessalonians did when Paul, Silas and Timothy first came to that pagan city preaching the gospel of Christ's death and resurrection.

Receive Him today and be ready. You have no assurance that you'll live another moment on this earth. You could die *before* you finish reading this paragraph. Furthermore, you have no assurance that Christ might not come this very moment—also *before* you finish reading this paragraph. Whether you die or whether you remain alive, you can—you should—be ready! Receive Jesus Christ today!

Remember the words of Paul in Romans 10:9-13:

> That if you confess with your mouth, "Jesus is Lord," and believe in your heart that God raised him from the dead, you will be saved. For it is with your heart that you believe and are justified, and it is with your mouth that you confess and are saved. As the Scripture says, "Everyone who trusts in him will never be put to shame." For there is no difference between Jew and Gentile—the same Lord is Lord of all and richly blesses all who call on him, for, "Everyone who calls on the name of the Lord will be saved."

Note
1. *Moody Alumni News,* n.d.

10

The Day of the Lord

1 THESSALONIANS 5:1-11

¹Now, brothers, about times and dates we do not need to write to you, ²for you know very well that the day of the Lord will come like a thief in the night. ³While people are saying, "Peace and safety," destruction will come on them suddenly, as labor pains on a pregnant woman, and they will not escape.

⁴But you, brothers, are not in darkness so that this day should surprise you like a thief. ⁵You are all sons of the light and sons of the day. We do not belong to the night or to the darkness. ⁶So then, let us not be like others, who are asleep, but let us be alert and self-controlled. ⁷For those who sleep, sleep at night, and those who get drunk, get drunk at night. ⁸But since we belong to the day, let us be self-controlled, putting on faith and love as a breastplate, and the hope of salvation as a helmet. ⁹For God did not appoint us to suffer wrath but to receive salvation through our Lord Jesus Christ. ¹⁰He died for us so that, whether we are awake or asleep, we may live together with him. ¹¹Therefore encourage one another and build each other up, just as in fact you are doing.

Both the Old and the New Testaments are filled with promises of the second coming of Christ. Someone has reported that there are 1,845 references in the Old Testament alone and a total of 17 books that give it prominence.

Of the 260 chapters in the entire New Testament, there are 318 references to Christ's second coming. That averages one out of every 30 verses. Furthermore, 23 of the 27 New Testament books refer to this great event. That leaves only four books that do not refer directly to the Second Coming. Interestingly, three of these four books are single-chapter letters which were written to specific persons on a particular subject.

Another interesting factor is that for every prophecy on the first coming of Christ—when He was born as a babe in Bethlehem—there are eight prophecies on Christ's second coming. These facts alone convince us of the extreme importance of the subject contained in 1 Thessalonians 5:1-11 and discussed in this chapter, "The Day of the Lord."

GOD'S JUDGMENT

The Thessalonian Christians were already well aware that Christ was going to come again. Paul affirmed this again as he began chapter 5 with these words: "Now, brothers, about times and dates we do not need to write to you, for you know very well that the day of the Lord will come" (1 Thess. 5:1-2). But the Thessalonian Christians were confused concerning certain details. That should not surprise us. Although we have God's complete written revelation in the Bible, it is still easy to be confused regarding certain aspects of this great event. One reason is that God has purposely not unveiled everything to us. But, there are certain things He has made very clear—and these we need to understand.

In a previous chapter, Paul, inspired by the Holy Spirit, clarified the issue of what happens to Christians who die before Christ returns. They and those who are still alive at this time "will be caught up . . . to meet the Lord in the air." Furthermore, Paul wrote, "We will be with the Lord forever" (4:17).

But what will happen next? These are the events Paul

reviewed for the Thessalonians in this opening paragraph in chapter 5. He dealt first with God's judgment on those people who will be alive when Christ returns, but who are not true believers in the Lord Jesus Christ.

Times and Dates—When Will Christ Return?

Note that Paul refers to "times and dates" (5:1). This can best be translated "times and seasons." He is not writing about actual 24-hour days or specific dates. Rather, he was referring to periods of time when certain events will take place. This is important because some well-meaning followers of Christ over the years have attempted to set specific dates.

One outstanding example involves William Miller, who was born in Pittsfield, Massachusetts, on February 15, 1782. He is often identified as the founder of the Seventh-Day Adventist movement, although there are several others who have affected the doctrinal teaching of this movement more than he.

All events point to the fact that William Miller was an upright, sincere Christian who believed in the reality of the second coming of Christ just as firmly as the Apostle Paul and the Thessalonian Christians did. Miller himself lacked formal theological training, yet along with many biblical scholars who *were* seminary graduates, he got caught up in a movement that taught that the second advent of Christ would take place sometime between 1843 and 1844. Using certain time references in the book of Daniel, they projected these dates. William Miller became quite specific and proclaimed that Christ would return sometime between March 21, 1843 and March 21, 1844. Those who followed Miller's prediction got caught up in frenzied excitement that turned into stark disappointment when this period passed without Christ's return to earth.

Miller confessed his error and acknowledged his disappointment. Yet he still believed that the day of the Lord was near and he exhorted Christians everywhere "to be watchful, and not to let that day come upon them unawares."[1]

Unfortunately, Mr. Miller did not learn the lesson all Christians should learn—that is, not to set specific dates for Christ's return. He endorsed what was then called "The Seventh-Month Movement." Its members became even more specific and set October 22, 1844 as the date for Christ's return. Many of those who had followed Miller's earlier theory once again were filled with ecstasy and hope.

But October 22, 1884, came and went, and these sincere but confused Christians were once again shattered and disillusioned. Miller himself died shortly after the second prediction failed to materialize, a brokenhearted man. Knowing what he believed about Jesus Christ, he went immediately to be with the Lord, but he left on earth many confused people, some of whom no doubt became disillusioned with Christianity altogether.

It is dangerous to set dates, even as some well-meaning people are doing today. Not only should we learn from Scripture that this should not be done, but we should learn from history.[2]

Day of the Lord—What Does This Mean?

In view of this kind of confusion, another concept that needs clarification in the minds of many Christians today is what the authors of Scripture meant by the phrase "the day of the Lord." In this passage, Paul is not referring to a specific 24-hour day. Rather, he was referring to a *time period* mentioned by many Old Testament prophets. One of these Old Testament prophets was Zephaniah. Speaking of this time period, he wrote:

> Near is the great *day of the Lord*,
> Near and coming very quickly;
> Listen, the *day of the Lord!*
> In it the warrior cries out bitterly.
> A *day* of wrath is that day,
> A *day* of trouble and distress,
> A *day* of destruction and desolation,
> A *day* of darkness and gloom,
> A *day* of clouds and thick darkness,
> A *day* of trumpet and battle cry,
> Against the fortified cities
> And the high corner towers (Zeph. 1:14-16, *NASB*).

In context it is clear that this Old Testament prophet is speaking of an extended period of time when God will judge the wicked directly and dramatically (see also Isa. 13:9-11). It is in contrast to what many identify as the "day of grace." This is the time period we are living in today. God in a special way is revealing His grace. Though God may choose to judge men and women today, He is long-suffering, as evidenced by the fact that He allows people to blaspheme His name.

Madalyn Murray O'Hair stands out as an unusual example. Many times she has shaken her fist at "God," asking Him to strike her dead if He exists. God in His grace, of course, has not responded to that request. But there will come a "day" when He will pour out His wrath and judgment on all those who have rejected His Son. Mrs. O'Hair, of course, does not realize that God's lack of response to her request is a reflection of His patience, love and grace.

Scoffers have always existed. They appeared on the scene early in church history. Peter spoke to this fact in his second Epistle. "You must understand," he wrote, "that in the last days scoffer will come, scoffing and following their own evil desires. They will say," Peter continued, "'Where is this "coming" he promised? Ever since our fathers died, everything goes on as it has since the beginning of creation'" (2 Pet. 3:3-4).

Peter then explains *why* Christ has not come and why He has not judged people like Mrs. O'Hair who challenge His existence. "But do not forget this one thing, dear friends," he wrote. "With the Lord a day is like a thousand years, and a thousand years are like a day. The Lord is not slow in keeping his promise, as some understand slowness. He is patient with you, not wanting anyone to perish, but everyone to come to repentance. But the *day of the Lord* will come like a thief" (2 Pet. 3:8-10).

Paul, then, like Peter, was referring to a time period when he wrote about the "day of the Lord" in his letter to the Thessalonians. Many believe that this period will begin when all Christians are raptured or "caught up" to be with the Lord—the event described in 1 Thessalonians 4:13-18. It appears to be an extended period of time lasting over a thousand years—including a time of tribulation on the earth and the actual coming of Christ to the earth to set up His millennial reign. It will seemingly culminate with what is described in Revelation 20:11-15 as the "great white throne" judgment.

Some Analogies of the Day of the Lord
What Will It Be Like?

After stating that the "day of the Lord" *will* come, Paul began to illustrate what it will be like. It will be "like a thief in the night" (1 Thess. 5:2), he explained. Here Paul expands on Peter's use of the same analogy. It is one thing to be robbed in broad daylight. It is quite another thing to be robbed at night. When Christ comes, many will be "asleep"—that is, totally unaware of what is happening.

Christ's return will also happen suddenly. As Paul stated in his second illustration, "While people are saying, 'Peace and safety,' destruction will come on them *suddenly,* as labor pains on a pregnant woman, and they will not escape" (5:3). The point, of course, that Paul was illustrating with this analogy is the suddenness, not the destructive aspects, of Christ's coming.

When our first child was being born, I stayed in the labor room all night with Elaine. Then when she went into the delivery room, I settled into the father's room and waited for another couple of hours. I thought the birth would never happen. But it did!

When Elaine became pregnant with our second child, I began preparing myself for the same lengthy ordeal. I remember Elaine awakened me about five in the morning. She had already been in labor for a couple of hours, walking around the house in a very relaxed state of mind getting ready to go to the hospital. She had been down this road before.

I jumped out of bed, got dressed and gathered up a stack of books and other materials to keep myself occupied. I must have gotten everything in order in about 15 minutes. But Elaine just kept taking her time as I paced nervously around the house. We finally got started for the hospital—a couple of hours later.

About halfway there her contractions began to come more

rapidly. Suddenly, *she* was nervous—especially since we were caught in a traffic jam several miles from the hospital. By the time we got there, they rushed her into the labor room and directed me to the father's room.

I walked into the room, piled my books on the table and began to study. Based on my past experience, I predicted I'd probably be waiting for at least another 8 to 10 hours. But, about five minutes later, the doctor appeared at the door. "Mr. Getz," he said, "you are the proud father of another baby girl." You can imagine my surprise! The *suddenness* of it all overwhelmed me.

Paul said the second coming of Christ will be *sudden*, "like labor pains on a pregnant woman." Not only will people not be expecting it, but the beginning of the day of the Lord will happen quickly.

GOD'S DELIVERANCE

First Thessalonians 5:1-3 emphasizes God's judgment on those who do not know Christ. But verses 4-10 emphasize that God will deliver from judgment those who are His children.

The Rapture—How Does It Relate to the Day of the Lord?

The term "rapture" is never used in the Bible. The word means to be "caught up" and is described in 1 Thessalonians 4:15-17. Many believe this specific event will begin the time period which is identified as the day of the Lord.

Views vary as to when the rapture will occur. Some say it will happen before the seven-year tribulation period which is associated with Daniel's seventieth week. Others believe it may happen in the middle of this period. Still others believe the rapture will happen after the seven-year period and simultaneously with Christ's actual coming to earth to set up His earthly Kingdom—a thousand-year period known as the millennium.

I personally believe the rapture will happen at the beginning of the seven-year tribulation period. This seems to me to be what Paul had reference to in 1 Thess. 5:9-10: "For God did not appoint us to *suffer wrath* but to receive salvation through our

Lord Jesus Christ. He died for us so that, whether we are awake or asleep, we may live together with him."

The terrible event that occurs during the tribulation period is that time when God pours out His wrath in judgment on mankind. These horrible judgments are described in detail in the book of Revelation. I personally believe Paul teaches that Christians will be in heaven during these events. God did not appoint us to suffer this wrath that will be poured out upon the earth.

The Raptured—Who Will They Be?

Paul used some very graphic and contrasting words to describe those who would be taken to heaven when the day of the Lord begins:

- They are "sons of the light"—not sons of "the darkness."
- They are "sons of the day"—not sons of "the night."

Note how Paul describes this contrast in 5:4-5: "But you, brothers, are not in darkness so that this day should surprise you like a thief. You are all sons of the light and sons of the day. We do not belong to the night or to the darkness."

Those who know Jesus Christ as personal Saviour need not fear the day of the Lord. Furthermore, this event should not take us by surprise. We should be constantly looking for His coming. True, we should not set dates. But we should understand that it could happen at any moment. As far as I understand the Bible, no significant things need to happen before Christ could come for His Church.

This expectation does not mean we should concentrate our efforts on looking and waiting. Rather, it means we should be about our Father's business, knowing that at any moment we could be caught up to be with Jesus Christ. It will be then that all of us as believers will appear before the judgment seat of Christ to give account of those things that we have done for Him here. We will be judged for our works—not in regard to our salvation, but in regard to the rewards that will be given by Jesus Christ Himself (see 1 Cor. 3:10-15).

PAUL'S EXHORTATION

In view of the fact that Christ could come at any moment, Paul admonished the Thessalonian Christians—and us—to do several things (1 Thess. 5:6-8,11).

"Be Alert"

In verse 6, Paul contrasts "alertness" with being "asleep." He is also teaching that as Christians we can become like non-Christians in our attitudes and actions. We can get so caught up in this world system that we lose sight of our eternal destiny.

This is particularly dangerous in the materialistic and entertainment-oriented world in which we live. Never before in the history of the world have we—particularly we Americans—had so many "things." We can become so enamored with the opportunities and challenges and pleasures of life that we begin focusing on ourselves rather than on why Christ left us on earth!

All Christians need constantly to evaluate their priorities in life. Let us not be lulled to sleep and become like the majority of the people around us.

"Be Self-controlled"

In verse 8, Paul used another illustration. He contrasted a state of self-control with a state of drunkenness. First he wrote, "For those who sleep, sleep at night, and those who get drunk, get drunk at night" (5:7).

Then Paul outlined how to be self-controlled in verse 8: "But since we belong to the day," he said, "let us be self-controlled, putting on

• faith and love as a breastplate, and the
• hope of salvation as a helmet."

With these three words, "faith," "hope" and "love," Paul was focusing on the true marks of maturity in a church. In a sense he was ending where he began. For Timothy had brought a report that the Thessalonians were indeed a maturing church. This is why Paul began this letter by thanking God for their "work produced by faith," their "labor prompted by love" and their "endurance inspired by hope" (1 Thess. 1:3).

With this exhortation to "be self-controlled," Paul was warning these Christians that it is possible to lose self-control as Christians. We must continually put on the "armor of God" (Eph. 6:11-18). Be assured that if there is a chink in our armor—as individuals or as a Church—Satan will make his move!

"Encourage One Another"

Being alert and self-controlled is a process we cannot achieve by ourselves. We need encouragement from other believers (1 Thess. 5:11). Knowing this truth makes it all the more important that we "not give up meeting together, as some are in the habit of doing, but let us encourage one another—and all the more as you see *the Day approaching*" (Heb. 10:25).

Here the author of the Hebrew letter is also referring to the day of the Lord. The longer we live, the more diligent we should be about meeting with other Christians to "build each other up" in our faith, in our hope and in our love.

The very week I was writing this chapter I met with a member of our own church. One of his major concerns was that he had neglected his responsibility to make sure his family attended church regularly. I was encouraged by his openness in his acknowledgment that, as a parent, he needed to set the example for his children.

One of the first things that happens in our world of opportunities and competitive activities is to neglect this important personal and family function. And when we do, we begin to lose our cutting edge as Christians. We can be lulled to sleep.

TWO CHALLENGES

There are many ways to encourage one another. *First,* do you know someone who used to be active as a Christian, attending church regularly and functioning as a part of the Body of Christ? Would you prayerfully approach that person immediately and lovingly share with him or her the need to be with God's people on a regular basis?

Let me exhort you not to feel you are imposing. Even if people do not respond, in their hearts they will appreciate your concern. Eventually they may respond. Don't let Satan intimidate you. Remember Paul's words to Timothy, "For God did not give us a *spirit of timidity,* but a spirit of power, of love and of self-discipline" (2 Tim. 1:7).

Recently I heard of a Christian leader who had separated from his wife. I had always looked up to this person and was shocked when I heard it. I decided to visit him as soon as possible. When I arrived at his home I discovered that he had essentially isolated himself from the outside world; he wouldn't even answer his phone. For nearly a year he had sat virtually alone suffering deep depression, hurt and fear.

I rang the doorbell twice—but there was no response. I was almost ready to turn and leave but decided to walk around to the back of the house. He had been outside, had not heard the doorbell and was very surprised to see me. I asked him if I could speak with him. Later he acknowledged that if I had not come upon him suddenly, he might not have let me in the door!

But in his heart he was moved that I took time to see him. In fact, he said that I was one of only a few people to make an effort during those long months. I tried to explain that all of us fear rejection or feel we may be imposing in situations like this. "But," I said, "the Bible teaches that 'perfect love casts out fear'" (1 John 4:18, *NASB*).

Remember that people may reject you outwardly but they may be crying out inwardly for help. Though their initial message may be mixed and confusing, they usually want someone to show concern.

My *second* challenge is, are you ready for Christ's return? More specifically, do you know Jesus Christ personally? If not, receive Him today and you will never need to fear the day of the Lord!

Notes
1. Sylvester Bliss, *Memoirs of William Miller* (New York: AMS Press, Inc., 1971, reprint of 1853 edition).
2. For a more thorough discussion of this issue see Walter R. Martin, *The Kingdom of the Cults* (Minneapolis: Bethany Fellowship, Inc., 1965), pp. 360-363.

11

Roles and Relationships

¹²Now we ask you, brothers, to respect those who work hard among you, who are over you in the Lord and who admonish you. ¹³Hold them in the highest regard in love because of their work. Live in peace with each other. ¹⁴And we urge you, brothers, warn those who are idle, encourage the timid, help the weak, be patient with everyone. ¹⁵Make sure that nobody pays back wrong for wrong, but always try to be kind to each other and to everyone else.

Someone has suggested five ways to get rid of your pastor:

1. Sit up front, smile and say "amen" every time he says something good. He will preach himself to death.

2. Pat him on the back and tell him what good work he is doing in the church and community. He will work himself to death.

3. Increase your offering in the church. He will suffer from shock.

4. Tell him you've decided to join the visitation group and win souls for the Lord. He will probably suffer a heart attack.

5. Get the whole church to band together and pray for him. He will get so efficient that some other church will hear about him and give him a call. That will take him off your hands.

Though said with tongue in cheek, these suggestions focus on an important subject—roles and relationships in the church. Paul spoke to this issue in 1 Thessalonians 5:12-15. As he began to draw this Epistle to a close, he dealt with two aspects of this subject: (1) relationships with spiritual leaders in the church and (2) relationships among members of the church; in short, relationships with one another.

RELATIONSHIPS WITH SPIRITUAL LEADERS

In 1 Thessalonians 5:12-13, Paul asked the believers in Thessalonica to have two basic attitudes toward their spiritual leaders—*respect* and *esteem*. But before we look at these attitudes and what they mean, notice the leadership responsibilities outlined by Paul.

Leadership Functions

1. "Those who work hard among you" (5:12).

Paul did not mention the *kind* of spiritual leaders he was referring to in the church at Thessalonica. Probably he was writing about elders since these were the first leadership positions filled in New Testament churches. For example, as Paul and Barnabas traveled together establishing churches in various cities on their first missionary journey, they eventually retraced their steps and "appointed elders for them in each church" (Acts 14:23). Since the church in Thessalonica was relatively new at the time Paul wrote his first letter to them, we would assume these were the men he had in mind.

On the other hand, it may be possible that there had emerged leaders in the church who had not been officially appointed. This, of course, happens in any social organization. There are those who are more highly motivated and begin to put in a great deal of time and effort. Perhaps this is why Paul first identified these leaders as "those who work hard among you."

2. *"Those . . . who are over you in the Lord" (1 Thess. 5:12).*

This statement implies that whoever these leaders were, they were recognized as having authority in the church. They were decision makers. If they were officially elders, this is understandable for this was their God-ordained task. They were to be overseers and managers. They were to "take care of God's church" (1 Tim. 3:1-5). This is why in other parts of Scripture they were alluded to as "shepherds" or pastors (Acts 20:28; 1 Pet. 5:2).

3. *"Those . . . who admonish you" (1 Thess. 5:12).*

The Greek word Paul used here and which is translated "admonish" is a very strong word. It literally means to "warn" people who are involved in doing things that are in violation of the will of God. When Paul met with the Ephesian elders he used this word to describe his dealings with those who "distort the truth" (Acts 20:30).

This same word now brings to focus a particular problem in Thessalonica. The role outlined for spiritual leaders in the church in other parts of Scripture is much broader than this specific kind of teaching; that is, "warning" or "admonishing" people. Pastoring and leading involves feeding the flock; encouraging God's people; praying for the sick (see James 5:14). Peter described their responsibility well when he said, "Be shepherds of God's flock that is under your care, serving as overseers—not because you must, but because you are willing, as God wants you to be; not greedy for money, but eager to serve; not lording it over those entrusted to you, but being examples to the flock" (1 Pet. 5:2-3).

Paul was dealing with a special need in Thessalonica. Evidently Timothy reported that some of these Christians were resisting the warnings being issued by their spiritual leaders. It may have related to "sexual immorality" (1 Thess. 4:3-6). It may have related to those who were not leading "a quiet life"; that is, they were not minding their "own business" and they were using their view of Christ's return to serve as a rationalization for their not working, making them financially dependent on others (4:11-12).

These were all problems that had to be dealt with in Thessalonica and it is easy to understand why the Christians who were violating these biblical principles may have resented spiritual guidance and warnings. This kind of resistance has existed throughout history and exists in every church today when biblical truth is taught.

When the Word of God cuts across areas in our life that are out of harmony with God's will, it is painful. Either we will respond to the truth in obedience or we will reject the truth. And sometimes, in rejecting the truth, we also reject those who teach the truth.

Attitudes Toward Spiritual Leaders

1. Respect

Paul instructed the Christians in Thessalonica to have two basic attitudes toward their spiritual leaders. The first was *respect*. "Now we ask you, brothers, to *respect* those who work hard among you, who are over you in the Lord and who admonish you" (5:12).

The concept Paul is expressing here is rather specific. It literally means "to know the worth" of these leaders or to "appreciate the value" of their efforts. If these leaders were truly "serving" these people, as they evidently were, and working very hard in the process, then they were to be highly valued and respected—not rejected, criticized or ignored.

There are various ways, of course, that this kind of attitude can be expressed by God's people. One is very tangibly described in Scripture in Paul's first letter to Timothy, who was appointing spiritual leaders in the church in Ephesus. Paul wrote, "The elders who direct the affairs of the church well *are worthy of double honor,* especially those whose work is preaching and teaching" (1 Tim. 5:17). The words "double honor" refer to financial remuneration, so we know that Paul here is referring to taking care of the material needs of those who give themselves primarily to ministry. The context, of course, makes this very clear, for Paul goes on to illustrate by saying, "For the Scripture says, 'Do not muzzle the ox while it is treading out the grain,' and 'The worker deserves his wages'" (v. 18).

The Bible makes it very clear that Christians who are ministered to spiritually should respond in a material way and care for those who serve them. Unfortunately, this is not a priority in many churches. In fact, surveys show that ministers on an average are considerably underpaid when compared with the income of the average person in a local congregation. Yet pastors put in far more time than that same average person.

I was interested in a survey conducted by Ministers Life and Casualty Union, an insurance company. The study was very thorough, taking in large, medium and small congregations and many denominations in both urban and rural settings. It was discovered that most pastors work seven days a week almost every week. They average nine hours a day, based on a seven-day week. The average work week was 53.7 hours. Those who interpreted the study pointed out that that is just two hours less than the average week put in by the chief executives of the top 500 U.S. corporations.

All of this points to the fact that most churches have a long way to go in being obedient to the Word of God in showing their "respect" to their spiritual leaders in a material way.

But taking care of a spiritual leader's material needs is not the only way to tangibly express respect. In fact, in many churches there are elders and other special leaders—as there are in ours—who are not staff leaders. Rather, they serve as lay leaders and devote hours of time and energy in carrying out their ministry to people.

In our own church we have small groups we call fellowship

families and minichurches. A fellowship family is an initial group of people who meet together regularly for a period of six months to study the Bible, to get to know one another and to have fellowship together. The minichurch is a permanent group that continues meeting together indefinitely, growing deeper in their relationship with God and one another. All of these groups are led by nonstaff pastors and their wives. It is in many respects a very demanding ministry, requiring hours of time that is invested in the lives of people.

These spiritual leaders do not expect financial remuneration. But they should be honored—in some cases more than those staff pastors who are remunerated. They not only spend hours on the job every day making a living, but they spend long hours ministering to people's spiritual needs in the church. Every Christian should honor and respect these people. They deserve words of praise and thanks!

Over the years I've seen nonstaff leaders in the church who have given hours of time, opened their homes and shared their material possessions, and yet very seldom have experienced any kind of reciprocal response. They are virtually taken for granted—both by the pastoral staff and by those they minister to! That, of course, should never happen in a church that calls itself Christian.

2. Esteem

The second attitude that should be demonstrated toward spiritual leaders is *esteem*. In a sense it is synonymous with an attitude of respect. Paul went on to elaborate when he said, "Hold them in the highest regard in love *because of their work*. Live in peace with each other" (1 Thess. 5:13).

Here Paul alludes to at least one other important factor. *Spiritual leaders are not perfect.* They make mistakes. But they should be esteemed nevertheless because of the very nature of the "work" they're doing.

Some Bible commentators believe that the spiritual leaders in Thessalonica had not handled some of the problems as sensitively as they should have. That, of course, is easy to understand. Even the leaders were relatively new believers. They, along with the other believers in the church, were in the process of growing in Christ and maturing in their Christian faith. And that, of course, has been true in every church since the first century.

Christian leaders do—and will continue to—make mistakes. And when it happens, they should not automatically lose respect or esteem. Christians should attempt to see beyond their human flaws and still appreciate their work and effort—even if it means respecting the fact that they are willing to put themselves in a vulnerable position of trying to help others. It's easy to throw stones when we are not in the position of responsibility. Rather, we should take this occasion to pray more intensely for our spiritual leaders.

This does not mean that spiritual leaders who sin against God and others should not be disciplined, and in some instances removed from their positions. James made it very clear that those who hold these positions will be held more accountable before God and "will be judged more strictly" (Jas. 3:1).

Paul spoke to this issue as well. First, he wrote Timothy not to accept an accusation against a spiritual leader "unless it is brought by two or three witnesses" (1 Tim. 5:19). There are people who become so angry at spiritual leaders that they will do anything to harm their reputation, including starting a malicious rumor, or even setting a trap for the person. This is why multiple witnesses are necessary.

But, if a spiritual leader *is* guilty of flagrant sin and violating the will of God, Paul made it clear that in those instances that person should be disciplined. "Those who sin," he wrote, "are to be rebuked publicly, so that the others may take warning" (1 Tim. 5:20). This instruction does not necessarily mean the sin should be revealed to everyone in the church. However, if the matter is public knowledge, that may need to be done.

RELATIONSHIPS WITH ONE ANOTHER

Paul spoke next about the responsibilities that all members of the local Christian body have toward each other. The spiritual leaders are responsible to give overall guidance to the church and to take a lead role in shepherding and teaching. But *every believer* is responsible to assist in carrying out the same basic functions. Paul outlined at least six (1 Thess. 5:14-15).

"Warn Those Who Are Idle"

As we've seen, idleness was a particular problem in the Thessalonian church. Some were *not* minding their own business. They were *not* working. Consequently, they became "busybodies" and evidently got into all kinds of trouble (2 Thess. 3:14).

Though it is difficult to do, sometimes the most effective exhortation comes from a very close friend and brother or sister in Christ. I know this is true in my own life. When someone confronts me who really knows and loves me, it gets my attention very quickly. It's always painful, but I know how vulnerable he or she is—and that is true love.

I remember approaching a superior on one occasion when I was a full-time professor. I was already close to this person. He was more than my boss—he was my friend. He had been conducting his affairs in such a way that it was alienating other teachers who reported to him.

I remember how much I struggled with the decision to finally share with him what was happening. Even though he was my friend, I feared rejection. More than that, I didn't want to hurt him.

After searching my own heart and motives, I finally got enough courage to communicate with him not only what was happening, but *why* I thought it was happening.

I was nervous. My voice quivered, my heart was pounding, and I had difficulty getting the words out of my mouth. But during that process he sensed my love for him, my vulnerability and my concern. The results overwhelmed me! It only proved to him that I *was* his friend. It resulted in a deeper relationship. He did not respond with anger but with gratitude.

"Encourage the Timid"

In most churches there are far more people who need to be

encouraged. They do not need criticism. They lack courage and emotional strength. They need a helping hand, a kind word, a pleasant smile and a warm touch. They need someone to say, "I believe in you! I'm your friend! I really care!"

Someone has said that for every negative statement, people need at least five or six positive comments to overcome the discouragement that results from negative feedback. Generally speaking, any negative input should always be preceded by positives and followed up with positives.

"Help the Weak"

Paul is speaking primarily of those who are struggling spiritually when he says to "help the weak." They are having difficulty living the Christian life. The temptations to sin seem more than they can bear.

Helping one another is one reason why groups such as Alcoholics Anonymous have been so effective. These people help each other. They model victory. And they are available to each other—to listen and to encourage—when the temptation to fall becomes overwhelming.

Should this not be true, and even more so in the church? And Paul is saying that every one of us in the Body of Christ is important if this is going to happen. In fact, it is only those who know us well who can even discern when we're having a struggle!

"Be Patient with Everyone"

Patience is a great virtue. It is the opposite of being short-tempered. If we're going to "encourage the timid" and "help the weak," it *will* take patience. People generally do not change their ways overnight. When tempted to give up on someone, think of God's patience toward you!

"Make Sure That Nobody Repays Wrong for Wrong"

This injunction is most difficult to apply. Our natural tendency is to say, "If you hurt me, I'll hurt you. I'll get even!"

This does not mean that sinful actions against us should not be confronted or dealt with. But we must follow God's procedure. And personal retaliation is never God's plan. Paul made this clear in his letter to the Romans when he wrote, "Do not repay anyone evil for evil . . . . Do not take revenge, my friends, but leave room for God's wrath, for it is written: 'It is mine to avenge; I will repay,' says the Lord . . . . Do not be overcome by evil, but overcome evil with good" (Rom. 12:17,19,21).

"Always Try to Be Kind to Each Other and Everyone Else"

This is really an extension of Paul's exhortation not to pay "back wrong for wrong." Jesus even included our enemies in this group. Speaking to the crowds on a mountainside one day, He said, "You have heard that it was said, 'Love your neighbor and hate your enemy.' But I tell you: Love your enemies and pray for those who persecute you" (Matt. 5:43-44).

I was stunned in the summer of 1984 when I heard that a young woman student at Moody Bible Institute in Chicago was murdered. Her badly beaten body was found under a pile of trash in an alley on North Wells Street, a short distance from the school. I was particularly moved by this incident because, both when I was a student at Moody Bible Institute and during the 13 years I served there as a professor, I walked that very street and passed thousands of times the exact spot where this terrible crime was committed. Startling also is the fact that this was the first time such a tragedy had happened in MBI's 100-year history—a miracle in itself, considering the environment in which many students minister throughout the Chicago area.

Kristen Kent was killed by a 29-year-old drifter named Larry Scott. Ironically, Kristen's brother-in-law had shared Christ with this man at Chicago's Pacific Garden Mission several months earlier. "I tried to show him the way of salvation," he said in one interview, "but he was as cold as ice."

Another aspect of this story is also very moving. Before her death, Kristen had written about her vision for ministering in the inner city. She wrote:

My impression of the inner city is that it is a dangerous place to live, full of crime and violence. It is a place where poverty prevails and sin is rampant .... I believe God is calling me to minister to the poor in urban America, first of all because my purpose here on earth is to glorify God (1 Cor. 6:20). In order to glorify God I am to obey Him (1 Pet. 1:14). Part of this obedience is to spread the Gospel (Acts 1:8) and to minister to the poor (Luke 10:30-37).[1]

But the point I'd like to make about this story is what Kristen's brother-in-law, Ed VonMeding, shared in an interview on a Chicago radio station. The interviewer asked Ed to describe his feelings toward the man who brutally killed Kristen as he robbed her. Holding back tears, Ed said, "I love him in Christ. It's hard to say, but Kristen would want me to say that and I know the Lord would. I want to have the opportunity to tell Larry Scott that."

Only God's love and strength could enable a man to maintain this spirit and attitude under such circumstances. Larry Scott was taken into custody. *He should pay for his crime.* But that responsibility belongs to the God-ordained authorities appointed by the state. Furthermore, God will have the final word regarding this man's eternal destiny. As Christians we should pray for his salvation so that he will face God as a redeemed man. This is what Paul is talking about in his letter to the Thessalonians when he wrote, "Make sure that nobody pays back wrong for wrong, but always try to be kind to each other and to everyone else" (1 Thess. 5:15).

SOME QUESTIONS FOR THOUGHT

1. Do you have proper *respect* and *esteem* for those who are over you in the Lord?
2. Have you in love reached out to those who are in direct violation of the will of God, warning them that they are in violation of God's commands?

Note: In doing so, we must make sure that we have practiced what God said. We are not to try to take a splinter out of our brother's eye when we have a huge plank in our own (Matt. 7:3-5). But we must be dealing with our own life and our own weaknesses as well (see Rom. 14:10-13; 15:14).

3. Are you encouraging the timid, the fearful and those who lack courage?

4. Are you helping those who are spiritually weak, reaching out a helping hand?

5. Are you patient with everyone, not allowing your temper to flare and hurt people?

6. Are you overcoming evil with good or are you attempting to personally avenge yourself against someone who has wronged you?

7. Are you demonstrating kindness to others on a regular basis—even those who may dislike you?

AN ACTION STEP

Read over these questions once again and select *one* that applies most directly to your life in relationship to another Christian—or in some instances to a non-Christian. Decide with God's help to act on the biblical exhortation your chosen question represents. Ask God to help you carry out this spiritual objective.

Note
1. *Moody Alumni Quarterly,* n.d.

12

Paul's Final Instructions

1 THESSALONIANS 5:16-28

[16]Be joyful always; [17]pray continually; [18]give thanks in all circumstances, for this is God's will for you in Christ Jesus.

[19]Do not put out the Spirit's fire; [20]do not treat prophecies with contempt. [21]Test everything. Hold on to the good. [22]Avoid every kind of evil.

[23]May God himself, the God of peace, sanctify you through and through. May your whole spirit, soul and body be kept blameless at the coming of our Lord Jesus Christ. [24]The one who calls you is faithful and he will do it.

[25]Brothers, pray for us. [26]Greet all the brothers with a holy kiss. [27]I charge you before the Lord to have this letter read to all the brothers.

[28]The grace of our Lord Jesus Christ be with you.

Someone has shared what they have described as "The Seven Wonders of the Word":

1. The wonder of its *formation*—the way in which it grew—one of the mysteries of time.

2. The wonder of its *unification*—a library of 66 books, yet one Book.

3. The wonder of its *age*—the most ancient of all books.

4. The wonder of its *sales*—the best-seller of all time and of any other book.

5. The wonder of its *interest*—the only book in the world read by all classes of people.

6. The wonder of its *language*—written largely by uneducated men, yet the best book from a literary standpoint.

7. The wonder of its *preservation*—the most hated of all books, yet it continues to exist.[1]

Paul's letter to the Thessalonians confirms these statements. As Paul concluded this Epistle, giving some final instructions to these relatively new believers, we see once again the wonder of Scripture. Paul concisely outlines at least 11 power-packed exhortations and injunctions—each one worthy of a complete chapter. Space prohibits our doing that, so let's look at each one briefly, yet in a meaningful way.

THREE UNUSUAL EXHORTATIONS

I've labeled these three exhortations *unusual,* because they are *unique* to Christianity. In fact, apart from Christian theology, they don't make sense. They are considered illogical and irrational by the average human being, and certainly not realistic. Let's look at each one individually and see why they are so unusual.

"Be Joyful Always"

"How is it possible to be joyful always?" you ask. Certainly this is a logical question. To comprehend what Paul means when he wrote, "Be joyful always" (1 Thess. 5:16), we need to understand that he is not talking about joy in the usual sense. He is not referring to a consistent emotional high. It *is* impossible and unrealistic to live on that plane. Furthermore, that kind of living would be harmful to us physically, since it is abnormal. God did not design the human body to tolerate excessive amounts of adrenalin being released into our physiological system—a phenomenon that invariably happens when we are experiencing unusual emotional excitement on a prolonged basis.

Emotions fluctuate, not only because of difficult situations, but due to physical drain that accompanies the normal responsibilities in life. So Paul here refers, not to some euphoric state, but to an unusual sense of contentment and inner peace that every Christian can experience in spite of life's circumstances, inner turmoil, grief, stress or even physical pain.

Paul testified to this reality in his own life in his second letter to the Corinthians. After outlining a series of incredible personal experiences: "in troubles, hardships and distresses; in beatings, imprisonments and riots; in hard work, sleepless nights and hunger" (2 Cor. 6:4-5)—he concluded his description with an amazing statement. We are "*sorrowful*", he wrote, "yet *always rejoicing*" (6:10).

This does not mean that a joyful response was automatic with Paul, nor does it mean it is automatic for any Christian. Writing to the Philippians from a Roman prison, Paul stated, "I *have learned the secret of being content* in any and every situation, whether well-fed or hungry, whether living in plenty or in want." Paul's secret? "I can do everything through him who gives me strength," he exclaimed (Phil. 4:12-13)! When facing circumstances that were at times unbearable and beyond his control, Paul drew inner strength from Jesus Christ.

To be "joyful always" is a supernatural experience that results when we look to God for help, see the good that can result from the experience and look beyond the present pain to envision the maturity that will result from particularly difficult situations. James had this perspective in mind when he wrote, "Consider it *pure joy,* my brothers, whenever you face trials of many kinds, because you know that the testing of your faith develops perseverance. Perseverance must finish its work so that you may be mature and complete, not lacking anything (Jas. 1:2-4).

"Pray Continually"

When Paul told the Thessalonians to "pray continually" (1 Thess. 5:17), he was not instructing these Christians to spend 24 hours a day talking to God. Rather, he was implying that it is possible to be in a constant spirit of prayer. Our very thoughts and concerns can be so focused on God that every desire of our heart is consistently in harmony with His will. Our very thoughts become prayer.

Being in a spirit of prayer does not mean that we must constantly be sober and somber. Even laughter and humor can be a setting in which our hearts are in tune with God. The very week I wrote this chapter I was ministering to a group of pastors on the West Coast. Just before I spoke one evening, four of these men did a humorous takeoff on preachers. I haven't laughed so hard for a long time. It was fun laughing at ourselves. As I stood up to speak, I could only thank God in my prayer before the message for the proverb, "A cheerful heart is good medicine" (Prov. 17:22).

I believe Paul was also making another point when he exhorted believers to "pray continually." He was simply saying, "Don't forget to pray on a regular basis. Make it a priority in your life."

And, of course, prayer becomes one of the secrets that enables us to receive inner strength and to be able to rejoice in the midst of difficult situations. Paul clearly integrates joy and prayer in his Philippian letter. Note how he blends the two elements in this passage:

> *Rejoice* in the Lord always. I will say it again: *Rejoice!* Let your gentleness be evident to all. The Lord is near. Do not be anxious about anything, but in everything, by *prayer* and *petition, with thanksgiving,* present your requests to God. And the *peace of God,* which transcends all understanding, will guard your hearts and your minds in Christ Jesus (Phil. 4:4-7).

"That sounds great!" you're tempted to say. "But, could Paul *really* practice this in his own life?"

Luke records an event that illustrates this experience, not only in Paul's life, but also in that of his companion Silas. Both were thrown in prison in Philippi where the Christians lived who received this Philippian letter. These missionaries had been severely beaten and locked up in the inner cell—the place reserved for hardened criminals. Their feet were fastened in stocks. In that setting, with blood still oozing from their wounds, they lifted their voices to God. "About midnight Paul and Silas were *praying* and *singing* hymns to God" (Acts 16:25).

Paul *did* practice what he preached. He *had* learned the "secret of being content" in all circumstances.

"Give Thanks in All Circumstances"

I had the privilege of writing an article for *Decision* magazine entitled, "You Don't Have to be Afraid of a Nuclear Holocaust." In that article I made reference to Paul's statement that we are to "give thanks in all circumstances" (1 Thess. 5:18). I further explained that to "give thanks *in* all circumstances" does not mean that a Christian has to "give thanks *for* all circumstances."

I received a letter from a dear lady who read the article. Referring to Paul's statement in 1 Thessalonians she wrote:

> This truth has been a mainstay in my life. I was married to a blind man for almost 34 years. During that time, we pastored churches until eight months before his death at 69—over 30 years. And 10 years ago he passed away and especially since that time I have aimed to thank God "for" and "in" those circumstances.

This lady's response indicates that there's a very fine line between thanking God "*in* all circumstances" and "*for* all circumstances." But I do believe there is a line. There are some things that happen that I don't believe God wants us to thank Him for. If we did, we would be thanking Him for evil. However, He always wants us to be thankful in the midst of any situation—thankful that He is in control of our lives, that He is with us, that He will never forsake us.

Paul culminates these three injunctions with the following statement, "For this is God's will for you in Christ Jesus" (5:18). It appears that Paul is relating this statement back to all three injunctions

- "Be joyful always."
- "Pray continually."
- "Give thanks in all circumstances."

The week before I began to research these unusual and unique exhortations, a member of my own church shared—in writing—an experience he had had with the Lord. I considered this to be providential, for what he has written illustrates beautifully the potential of being able to apply all three of these injunctions in our lives. He wrote:

> I woke up early this morning as I have been doing for many weeks now, too early really, but I couldn't sleep any more—too many things were burdening me and causing my mind to be troubled. My wife's physical problem continued to bother her and other responsibilities were weighing on my mind. But most of all, the pressure at work seemed almost unrelenting. As I quieted my heart before the Lord, He impressed on me that there were some things I needed to face about my reaction to all of this.
>
> *Forgiveness*
> I needed to forgive everyone who was making my life pressured—my kids, my wife, my students, my job, the boss—any and all of them. I needed to forgive them freely and let go of that resentment that was stewing within.
>
> *Self-pity*
> Like quicksand, [self-pity] had been pulling me

lower and lower. I confessed the sin of self-pity. I did this knowing it was the key before I could overcome my depression.

Surrender

I'd been holding back, not totally willing to be and do anything that God wanted me to. I needed to give up my own will and want God's.

Trust

I had forgotten the simple yet profound assurance from Psalm 23, "The Lord is my Shepherd, I shall not be in need." I'd forgotten that God was sufficient. I didn't have to have the power and resources in myself. I turned again back to God. I just saw again what I'd seen so often, without Him I can do nothing; I can't make it by myself. With Christ living through me, I can make it.

Joy

With these things settled and with my trust back in God, I was happy again. I could sing, "Praise the Lord, Alleluiah. I don't care what the devil's going to do!" The Word and faith were once again my sword and shield. And Jesus was the Lord of the way I feel.

My attitudes have changed and with them my feelings as I have decided to let go (of my unforgiveness, self-pity, and self-will) and to let God take over. It's really trust in Him and not myself.

"I'm now happy in You, Lord," I prayed, "not because of my circumstances, but because of *who You are* and because I trust in You to be the *Lord* of my life and my circumstances."

The person who wrote this included a footnote which reads, "I shared this material with my wife and she was also happy. 'There's been a heavy cloud over you and now it's gone,' she said. 'It's good to have my old honey back again.'"

SOME BALANCED CAUTIONS

In 1 Thessalonians 5:19-22, Paul outlined five succinct cautions for the Thessalonian Christians. In order to understand his concern, we need to look at all of these in concert:

- "Do not put out the Spirit's fire."
- "Do not treat prophecies with contempt."
- "Test everything."
- "Hold on to the good."
- "Avoid every kind of evil."

One of the ways God communicated with New Testament believers was by the gift of prophecy. For example, when Paul was on his way to Jerusalem he stayed at Philip's house in Caesarea. Luke records that "a prophet named Agabus came down from Judea." In order to communicate a message he had received from God, "he took Paul's belt, tied his own hands and feet with it and said, 'The Holy Spirit says, "In this way the Jews of Jerusalem will bind the owner of this belt and will hand him over to the Gentiles"'" (Acts 21:10-11).

This, of course, was a correct message. It happened as Agabus said it would. A true prophet was enabled by the Holy Spirit to predict the future with total and absolute accuracy. In fact, this was to be the test of a true prophet in the Old Testament. To claim falsely to be a prophet in Israel was punishable by death (Deut. 18:20-22).

As in the Old Testament, there were those in the New Testament who claimed to have the gift of prophecy and to receive messages from God. But they were not true prophets. Their messages were not authentic. But since this gift existed, Paul warned these Christians not to stand in the way of what the Holy Spirit wanted to communicate through a particular member of the church. They were not to have a negative attitude toward prophetic messages.

However, Paul warned them to test what was communicated very carefully and to respond only to that which was good. In saying that, Paul indicated there were some who spoke so-called "messages" from God but they are not good. Rather, they are evil. In fact, they could be inspired by Satan. Thus Paul warned against that possibility.

This raises a very important question. Is this gift operative today? There is disagreement among many Bible teachers on this issue. My personal opinion is that this gift was operative primarily during the first century while Christianity was becoming established and the New Testament Scriptures were coming into existence. However, we must remember that God can do anything He wants at any moment in history. Thus Paul's cautions to the Thessalonian Christians are still applicable today.

My own experience is that most of what I have heard as "prophetic utterance" today does not have the ring of authenticity when compared with the prophecies that took place in the New Testament when this gift was exercised. Today, it is often a repetition of Scripture or is so general in nature that what is predicted does indeed come to pass—and most people know from experience what is going to happen anyway.

It is also easy to be self-deceived in these areas. While I was writing this chapter a pastor friend told me of a man in his congregation who claimed to have this gift and sent him what he claimed was a letter from God. It turned out that the man, though normal in many respects, had a history of psychological difficulties. No one questioned this man's sincerity, but he was obviously confused. He was taking what was a New Testament gift and simulating that gift in his own mind.

Another man distributed a letter throughout Southern California during the 1984 Olympics, claiming that God told him that a great earthquake was going to hit the Los Angeles area during that period of time. However, he also indicated that God told him that if people repented of their sins the earthquake would not take place. Woven throughout the letter were Old Testament Scriptures—taken out of context—to demonstrate that this was a message from God (incidentally, this was not the first time this man had sent out letters which he claimed were prophetic messages).

The earthquake did not happen. And anyone who was in Southern California during the Olympics is well aware of the fact that there was no significant repentance for sin. If anything, there was probably more sinful living than normal taking place by those who had come to observe this international event.

All of this points to the fact that we must be very cautious about listening to people who claim to have a message from God. We must "test everything" very carefully, but at the same time be very cautious that we do not interfere with the work of God's Holy Spirit.

A PRAYER FOR TOTAL SANCTIFICATION

It is not accidental or surprising that Paul follows these cautions about prophecy with a prayer for growth and maturity. This is the emphasis of the New Testament. Nowhere are we, as individuals, told to seek for or to attempt to discover our spiritual gifts. Rather, we are told again and again to become mature in Jesus Christ. This is what Paul meant here by "sanctification": "May God himself, the God of peace, *sanctify you through and through.* May your *whole spirit, soul and body* be kept blameless at the coming of our Lord Jesus Christ. The one who calls you is faithful and he will do it" (1 Thess. 5:23-24).

The Thessalonian Christians were well on their way toward Christian maturity—both corporately and personally. This is one reason why Paul began this letter by thanking God for their "work produced by *faith,*" their "labor prompted by *love,*" and their "endurance inspired by *hope*" (1:2-3). When Paul wrote a letter to a church he was pleased with in terms of their spiritual growth, he would often begin the letter by thanking God for these three qualities in that particular church (see Eph. 1:15,18; Col. 1:3-5; 2 Thess. 1:3).[1]

SOME CONCLUDING INJUNCTIONS

The three injunctions at the end of this letter are not particularly related. One is a personal prayer request. Another emphasized the importance of demonstrating affection and love to each other and the third exhorted these believers to share the message of this letter with all the Christians in Thessalonica and the surrounding area.

"Brothers, Pray for Us"

Paul seldom focused on his own needs. However, he always acknowledged his need for prayer (1 Thess. 5:25). And often his prayer request focused on the need to be faithful to the Lord in sharing the gospel. For example, in writing to the Ephesians, he requested the following very personal petition: "Pray also for me, that whenever I open my mouth, words may be given me so that I will fearlessly make known the mystery of the gospel, for which I am an ambassador in chains. Pray that I may declare it fearlessly, as I should" (Eph. 6:19-20).

"Greet All the Brothers with a Holy Kiss"

First Thessalonians 5:26 is one of five such exhortations in the New Testament (see also Rom. 16:16; 1 Cor. 16:20; 2 Cor. 13:12; 1 Pet. 5:14). The important issue in this exhortation is not the *form* of the greeting, but rather the meaning behind the greeting. The way in which people express love and affection varies from culture to culture. But whatever that greeting, it should always be a *holy* expression and meaningful.

I remember one occasion when I walked into the church and greeted a young high school student named Bruce. I asked him how he was doing. About a minute later, one of the elders tapped me on the shoulder and told me he wanted to admonish me in love. He had overheard my greeting to this young man.

"What did I do?" I responded.

He reviewed the scenario for me. "You asked Bruce," he said, "how he was doing. But you did not stay around long enough to hear his answer."

At this juncture, of course, this elder had my undivided attention. "What did he say?" I asked.

"Well," he responded, "when you asked him how he was doing, he responded by saying, 'Not very well. My brother was in a motorcycle accident today.'"

My heart sank. I realized that in my busyness and preoccupation with other things, I had asked him how he was doing, but I was exercising a ritualistic greeting. I had not really intended in my heart to find out the answer to that question. I'm thankful that a sensitive elder overheard the conversation and admonished me so that I could go back and ask forgiveness. And, of course, the young man readily forgave me.

The important message in this injunction, then, is that when we greet people, we should do so sincerely. We should avoid getting caught in meaningless protocol. Christians of all people should be sincerely interested in one another and express that interest in a culturally acceptable way.

"Have This Letter Read to All the Brothers"

At this point (5:27), review the introduction to this chapter. The focus is on the uniqueness of Scripture. Though this letter was indeed written first and foremost to the Thessalonians, it is a part of God's holy Word. Consequently, it is just as relevant today as it was during the first century. As pastors and teachers, may we not neglect sharing the contents of this letter with our congregations. And as individual Christians, may we not neglect to read it personally and apply its truths to our own lives.

A FINAL BENEDICTION

After telling the Thessalonians to "have this letter read to all the brothers" (5:27), Paul gives his final benediction: "The grace of our Lord Jesus Christ be with you" (5:28).

And that is also my prayer for you that the grace of our Lord Jesus Christ be with you.

Notes

1. Paul Lee Tan, *Signs of the Time* (Rockville, MD: Assurance Publications), 1979.
2. Compare the introduction and specific exhortations in the letters to the Ephesians, the Colossians, and the Thessalonians with the letter that was written to the Corinthians. In the Corinthian letter Paul did not thank God for faith, hope, and love. Rather, he thanked God for their gifts, but then proceeded to exhort them regarding their carnality and immaturity (1 Cor. 1:4-7; 3:1-3). Later in chapter 13, Paul emphasized faith, hope, and love (see the context of 1 Cor. 13:13). Though he did not forbid the Corinthians to use their gifts, he exhorted them to follow the way of love first and foremost. For an extensive study of how the concepts of faith, hope and love are used in the New Testament see Gene Getz, *Measure of a Church* (Ventura, CA: Regal Books, 1975).